BRICK LANE: *Bari to Basa*

Shahagir Bakth Faruk M.Sc, FRSPH

In the name of Great Gracious, Glorious and Generous God, the Almighty, the All-wise, the All-Gentle, the All-Compassionate, the All-Knowing Allah-the most Merciful, the most Magnificent, the most Beneficent.

ISBN 978-0-9928533-5-8

Cover Design: Maisha Bakth

Edited by Jan Andersen
http://www.creativecopywriter.org

PERFECT PUBLISHERS LTD
23 Maitland Avenue
Cambridge
CB4 1TA
England
http://www.perfectpublishers.co.uk

Dedication in Warm Remembrance

This book is dedicated to those who have loving memories of Brick Lane and also to those from Brick Lane who have passed away.

'I feel lonely when I go to Park Lane, but feel homely when I come back to Brick Lane.'

Contents

Preface

John Eade
Professor of Sociology and
Anthropology, University of
Roehampton; Member of the
Migration Research Unit,
University College London;
Visiting Professor, Dept for
the Study of Religion,
University of Toronto

It is a great pleasure to endorse this book. Shahagir Bakth (Faruk) and I belong to the same generation and in our different ways we have seen how the British Bangladeshi settlement has developed since the late 1970s. We have both focused on the heartland of the Bangladeshi community – the London borough of Tower Hamlets – and the ways in which Brick Lane in particular has expressed, both physically and symbolically, the rapid changes that have taken place during our lifetime.

Faruk wants to celebrate the many and varied achievements of his fellow Bangladeshis, not only in Brick Lane and Tower Hamlets, but also across London and towns and cities beyond the metropolis. This is an important move because Bangladeshis for a long time have been associated with urban poverty and low achievement. Clearly, the socio-economic problems that Bangladeshis encountered during the 1980s and 1990s have moderated. A significant number from the younger generation 'born and bred' in Britain have made their way through the educational system to university and into middle class occupations. An hour glass is perhaps the best image to describe the contemporary Bangladeshi socio-economic situation. The lower part of the hour glass bulges with the large number of people who are still affected by unemployment, poor housing and health problems. Yet, the other end is expanding through the rising middle class which Faruk seeks to celebrate here.

These socio-economic changes have been accompanied by striking political and cultural changes. My own research sought to analyse an important shift in political representation, as younger activists during the early 1980s engaged with the British political mainstream more deeply than their elders. As Faruk points out, this process has led to the emergence of a wide range of political representatives. At the same time, cultural developments – especially involving Islam – have brought the local and the global community together through, for example, the building of mosques and madrassahs, campaigns around food and clothing and engagement with geopolitics involving Muslims around the world. This interweaving of cultural and political processes also shapes the continuing, if changing, relationship between Bangladeshis in Britain and their country of origin.

The title of this book – Brick Lane: *Bari to Basa* – seeks to represent the movement from Bangladeshi to British ways and the achievements that some Bangladeshis at least have experienced. The move from bari (home) to basa (house) is a complex process as the developments outlined above indicate. Bangladeshis and others, who share a recent migration history, are tied by transnational bonds, which hold the bari and basa together. These bonds are experienced differently according to generation, but even those brought up in Tower Hamlets and elsewhere in Britain retain some tie with their family's country of origin, however attenuated.

We live in a highly connected world where events in one country can quickly impact on others far away, as the recent massive increase in migration flows across the Mediterranean illustrates. This is a world that we need to explore through the first-hand accounts of those who closely inhabit it. Hence, the significance of this book and others hopefully to emerge in the not-too-distant future.

Book Reviews in Alphabetical Order

**Dr A K Abdul Momen
Bangladesh Ambassador
and Permanent
Representative to the UN**

I am thankful to Mr Shahagir Bakth Faruk, a very proactive college friend of mine, for sending me his manuscript of Brick Lane. He has been a part and parcel of Brick Lane for years and he not only knows all the bricks of Brick Lane, but also its contemporary history, its ugly side of racism, its wonderful accomplishments, its ups and downs and its upgradation from a run-down inner city slum to an upscale development zone.

In the early 1970s, when I used to visit Brick Lane, it was an English and Jewish neighbourhood of fabric traders that later turned into a Bangladesh enclave, a nucleus of all Bangladeshi activities; politics, cultural and religious festivities, economic and trade activities and, more importantly, homeland of authentic Bangladesh cuisine (known as Indian cuisine) where one would not be surprised to see a man wearing lungi in a British land. Now it is the world's Curry Capital and, more importantly, home of a vibrant Bangladesh Diaspora – Bangla City, the epicentre of Bangla accomplishment throughout the UK. Nowadays when I visit it, I call it 'My Second Home'– second home of Sylhetis of Bangladesh.

The British ruled us for years and its poet Rudyard Kipling once wrote, 'The East is East, The West is West, and never the twain shall meet'. Now the Brick Lane has made him questionable; the twain can meet and can enjoy each other's company and cuisine. Their values and aspirations are not hostile any longer, but rather merging and blending together.

I was thrilled at the topics that Faruk put up such as, 'From Thousand Miles to Thousand Smiles', 'Work, Women and Weather', 'Place, People and Politics', 'Associations, Awards and Accolades', 'Family, Festivals and Fun', 'Peaceful Place for Praying People', or 'Bari to Basa'. These topics enticed me to go over them, although I have very limited time.

I commend Faruk for his creativity, his rhythmic innovativeness and the lucid way of his narration. No wonder, it reminds me that he is from the land of Hason Raja, the legendary gayok of Sunamganj of Bangladesh whose words of wisdom and music are eternal.

A few years ago when I had the privilege to read Nurul Islam's book on Probashi or Bangladesh Diaspora in the United Kingdom, I was thrilled, as it was a well-researched book on Bangladeshi immigrants in the UK. However, Shahagir's book is a reflection of the contemporary running note of Brick Lane and its Bangladesh immigrant community that will, hopefully, be a rich addition to the ever changing life and living of Bangladeshi Diaspora in the United Kingdom. Secondly, if you forget the names of your old friends or accomplices of England, this book can help you to refresh your memory and can enrich your life.

I wish him success and I shall be pleased if this book helps our new generations to understand their roots, their sacrifices, their achievements and be proud of their heritage, their present and the past. Let them be proud of their land of origin, Bangladesh, which turned itself from a 'basket case with no hope of survival' to a 'model of economic development'. As per the Wall Street Journal, 'a standard bearer of the South', a land of vibrant economy that has been successful in reducing poverty more than half, is on track to achieve most of the Millennium Development Goals and has become, as per Goldman Sachs' next Emerging 11, a land of opportunities, or

Bangabandhu's dream, a Sonar Bangla or Golden Bengal.

Dr Abul Kalam Azad
Editor, Monthly Zaitun Magazine
and Executive Director, Cambridge
Research Academy, London

I was truly honoured by Prof Shahagir Bakth Faruk, a prominent British Bangladeshi social activist and businessman, when he asked me to write down some comments on his book on Brick Lane.

Prof Faruk has explained the nature of his book by saying, 'This book is not like Monica Ali's Brick Lane nor similar to Ansar Ullah or Phil Maxwell's books on Brick Lane. This is about a home from home. It's about success stories of Bangladeshis.'

Brick Lane is a cultural icon for London, which is predominantly enriched by British Bangladeshis. Although Brick Lane is known to many people as 'Bangla Town' or 'Curry Capital', a non-Bengali blogger mentioned, 'Brick Lane is above all a social hub – whether through its rich history of international communities coming together here, or whether through its independent café culture, cuisine, the Sunday market, a shared appreciation of the arts and the nightly explosion of trendy clubbers and buzzing barflies.'

Another blogger wrote: 'To be honest, I am pretty mainstream; I've never owned a retro denim jacket that smells like a charity shop, but nevertheless I love it here. A little because everybody here is cooler than me and also because there is nowhere else quite like it in London.'

So, Brick Lane is a unique 'mini town' in London, which has every reason to attract a writer like Prof Faruk.

In the same way, Prof S B Faruk has been able to capture the global dynamics of Brick Lane in this book. However, in his eye-witness accounts, he mainly tries to focus on first and second generations of British Bangladeshis who have contributed to the British society in different ways, including media, business, culture and politics.

Prof Faruk is known to us as a lovely and very humble person, and these attributes were clearly reflected in this book, when he said, 'I have tried to pencil these memories in this paper book and for obvious reasons while putting all these memories together, it is not unusual to make errors. I hope the readers will excuse my inadvertent mistakes.'

While I read it, I had the feeling that Brick Lane is so deeply rooted in his mind and head that any reader can easily give him a title 'The

Brick Lane Man'. Prof Faruk 'since his very first day in England, fell in love with the people and the country'. This suffices to say that Prof Faruk is a 'living and genuine' example of 'British Bangladeshis' whose love and dedication for both countries is very honest and sincere.

With his positive mind, Prof Faruk rightly opined, 'I strongly believe that if there is cooperation, coordination and collaboration among the organisers and harmony and brotherhood relationships among the caterers, many of its problems could easily be resolved slowly and gradually, but surely and certainly.'

I believe the facts and figures he presented here are authentic and impartial. His academic backgrounds make him balanced in emotive descriptions and fairness of the events and incidents in and around Brick Lane. I, therefore, believe this book will be well received by the readership and researchers as a reliable source on Brick Lane and its Bangladeshi communities.

I thoroughly enjoyed reading this book and hope others will enjoy it too.

I would recommend this valuable history based autobiography for our British Bangladeshi young generations who may sometimes experience an identity crisis.

I wish Prof Faruk a long life and good health.

Anne Main, MP

I found *Brick Lane: Bari to Basa* to be a valuable insight into the changing social landscape of Brick Lane.

Brick Lane and the east of London have changed immensely since the war. It has become a thriving multi-racial hub of cultural activity, and its turnaround is testament to the hard work of those who have settled there.

As the chair of the All-Party Parliamentary Group on Bangladesh, I am acutely aware of how Bangladeshis have settled in the UK, and their immense pride in both their old and new home. British-Bangladeshis like Faruk have come to the UK, worked hard, settled and greatly contributed to the British way of life.

'I have known Faruk for many years, and it is easy to see why he is a well-known and influential gentleman in the Brick Lane area.

Enam Ali MBE, FIH
Publisher, Editor of Spice Business
Magazine and Founder of the
British Curry Awards

Shahagir Bakth Faruk is someone I have known for over two decades and I have witnessed first-hand his unprecedented contribution to our community, including his passion for social welfare, politics and hospitality training. Many curry houses around the country respect him for his support.

Faruk's new book, Brick Lane: Bari to Basa, expresses his emotions and experiences from the very first day he arrived in the UK in 1973 until today. He has written perfectly about his 41 years' experience of his life as a foreigner up to being a loyal proud Bangladeshi-British citizen. He sums it up well when he says, 'I feel lonely when I go to Park Lane, I feel homely when I come back to Brick Lane.'

He has elaborated his nostalgia, his experience of racial hatred and of living in fear, but has also covered immigrant success and economic and social transformation. He does this with the reference of hundreds of people in Britain, mainly Bangladeshi immigrants, whose contribution has made what Britain is today.

This book warrants the 'must read' label, as an immigrant's recipe for success with true ingredients. Reading this will show the next generation how to understand our values and how we moved from being foreigners to finding home sweet home in the East End of London.

He also turns his political eye on Britain and recalls his time as a Conservative candidate when he stood in the Bethnal Green and Bow election in 2001 and 2005. He has made a big contribution to engaging the community with this political party and was a pioneer in forming the Conservative Friends of Bangladesh.

Writing this book movingly and perfectly, with so many true incidents, makes it a huge success. Certainly our community will feel a sense of pride through his experience and knowledge.

I hope a world audience will be inspired while reading this book at this critical time in history of the world, where millions people are being displaced for many reasons. I would like to congratulate him on publishing such a wonderful book and wish him every success in his journey.

Shahida Rahman
Author, Writer and Publisher

Shahagir Bakth Faruk paints a colourful story of his life in Brick Lane. He is a well-respected member of the British Bangladeshi community.

For centuries the East End has been the first port of contact for many immigrants working in the docks and shipping from East India. It is the heart of the city's Bangladeshi-Sylheti community and is famous for its market and numerous curry houses.

Shahagir is an inspiration to many and his remarkable life story tells of the many challenges he faced living and working in the Brick Lane area. It is important to remember the hard work of our forefathers and these stories need to be told. He has portrayed Brick Lane positively as a symbol of success and a place of inspiration.

An interesting read for anyone who wants to find out more about the changing face of Brick Lane.

Taysir Mahmud
Editor, Weekly Desh, London

This book is a wonderfully written personal account of the history of Bangladeshi migration to Tower Hamlets. While reading this book, I felt I was transported back into 1970's Brick Lane. Mr Shahagir Bakth Faruk's descriptions of the area were very vivid and I could literally feel I was walking the streets of Tower Hamlets in his shoes.

This book will be an invaluable historical resource for future generations, to learn and understand about what it was like for first generation Bangladeshis in East London.

Foreword
Baroness Pola Uddin

Our transit through this century's history of Brick Lane has extraordinary tales of courage, commitment and audacity. Professor S B Faruk vividly recites his personal account amidst the transformative participation of the Bangladeshi community, its emerging young leaders working hand-in-hand with trade unions and the labour movements. The struggle ensued for its very survival, as the fascists bid to claim its tenure, and put in the danger the livelihood of many hundreds of new families who lived and worked in and around the Lane. The countless meetings, protests and marches to counter the fascists provided a common platform for unity of purpose and which provoked massive social change, culminating in a revival of the area unseen for hundreds of years. Its endurance rises out of the dreams and aspirations of a whole generation of activists, who not only took up the mantle to challenge institutional racism, but also contributed to shaping its very fabric, its education, housing, health and ultimately its governance.

Brick Lane is our generational centre of universe; it embodies our presence and it binds us together with all those hundreds of thousands of age old migrants who trod its path, with hopes and aspiration of a better life for their children and families. It stands today, etched with blood, sweat, toil and tears of our parents. In these early days, we were able to create a sense of belonging to Brick Lane. The author has encapsulated the complexities and vibrancy of Brick Lane with his personal and insightful experience.

Today's children are not privy to the pain and hard graft of their parents in making Brick Lane and the surrounding areas a home. Professor Faruk pays homage to the many individuals and their relentless efforts and sacrifices, so that we can call Brick Lane, Bangla Town and Tower Hamlets our home. Indeed, he is hopeful that his book will energise emerging activists of this era, to take up the responsibility for its future.

It's an excellent reference point for so many of us who devoted so much of our early adulthood seeking a just and fair society - each road, each building referred to in the book is imprinted in our minds and hearts. I am not so certain that I hold out the author's vision of tomorrow's Brick Lane and the surrounding area, given that the regeneration of the area has so little impact on taking the vast section of the community out of poverty and at the same time pricing our kids out of the area.

Brick Lane of today also encounters a new set of challenges constructed within the counter terrorism, post 9/11 narrative, whilst there is a stark absence of strong movement that can successfully defend or challenge the ongoing demonisation and Islamophobia. Yes, we have better homes to live in, education and healthcare has improved immensely and there are a handful of home grown leaders. However, in truth, well paid jobs within our formal institutions and corporate organisations remain inaccessible for our children's generation and it is a fact that equal opportunities remain a paper exercise for many of these large and small employers. Many more of our children who are now graduates, cannot hope to occupy the vast array of professional jobs created on our doorsteps, because they are filled by those who commute into the Borough.

Even the housing and regeneration sectors – where the activists of the late 70s and early 80s contributed so much to the development – are still controlled primarily by white individuals, with one or two Bangladeshis to make up the numbers. It is a regrettable fact that most senior jobs of any importance remain firmly in the grip of same white, often male leaders. Many aspiring political leaders have been thwarted in a small way by internal division, but most significantly by colonialists and institutional racists, who continue their strategy of 'divide and rule' those few individuals of Bangladeshi heritage who were able to propel themselves to higher office.

Bangladeshis in powerful positions and high office have always been feared and derided in equal measure and this is the most profound tragedy for Brick Lane's British born Bangladeshi population in particular and for Tower Hamlets and its future. So, the ambitious who have echoed in every street in and around Brick Lane about the right of self-determination to lead our community, is only half the story.

It is of course great to be reminded of how much our home and the environment has changed and improved. The book reminds us of how dangerous the surrounding area was for Bangladeshis; it brings alive the vivid memory of the fascists and the fact that we can never fail to ensure that our children's and grandchildren's generation stay firmly rooted in the home that we built with love and sheer hard work.

Throughout the pages you can feel Professor Faruk's love and passion for Brick Lane. If I ever choose to pen a book, I will definitely re-read this again for reference.

Thank you, our Faruk bhai.

Author's Abstract Article

My home town Sunamganj in Bangladesh has a number of pathways, terraces, cul-de-sacs and narrow roads to describe and demarcate different type of public ways, but surprisingly none of them have 'Lane' at the end of their names. However, Sylhet – a bigger town 42 miles away from my home town – is known to have only one lane called 'Puran Lane'. Whereas Dhaka, the capital city of Bangladesh, has hundreds of lanes and in ancient days it was renowned for its 53 lanes and 52 bazaars. Even long before the independence of Bangladesh, a comedy film was made in (then) East Pakistan involving a lane, called Number 13 Feku Ostagar Lane.

Before coming to the UK in 1973, little did I know of any lane in England, let alone 'Brick Lane'. However, I always knew that 'lane' was used to describe the size of a small road, but after coming to London and visiting Brick Lane, Chancery Lane, Park Lane, Ilford Lane, Vicarage Lane, Turnpike Lane and many other lanes, it changed my perception. Park Lane rather looks like a big highway, motorway or dual carriageway with multiple lanes. On the other hand, I used to think that 'street' was nothing but a bigger version of a road. Downing

Street, leading to the official residence of the British Prime Minister, is too small and short, while 'Osborn Street' leading to Brick Lane is even shorter and smaller than Brick Lane.

Nevertheless, Brick Lane is not to be measured by length or width. It is now measured for its name and fame, image, honour, respect, reputation, diversity, strength, history and heritage, culture and custom, trade and traditions, curry houses and curry festivals, pageants and parades. Brick Lane is not only a trendy multicultural lane, but also a famous place for transformations, developments and regenerations that took place here. Now the south side of the lane is a place of almost hundred percent Bangladeshis.

Brick Lane has attracted the Bangladeshi community like a whirlpool. It is an epicentre of Bangladeshi community activities. Brick Lane is now a homogeneous area dominated by a vast majority of Bangladeshi Sylheti conglomerates. It has ancient houses, old flats, English Heritage buildings, modern bars, modern curry houses, variety offices and a mix of different communities where 102 languages are spoken in the Borough's schools alone.

Brick Lane has also built up a brotherhood relationship between Britain and Bangladesh. She has brought Bangladesh and Britain closer to each other. Brick Lane is very close to my heart for many reasons. I have seen her from close proximity. I made my cash and connections and campaigned from Brick Lane. I lived, listened and learnt through various community activities and involvement in Business and politics from Brick Lane. I am a witness of the gradual end of textile houses and the emergence of curry houses. I witnessed how cinema and audio/video businesses closed down slowly and gradually in front of my own eyes. I saw the faces of enmity, hatred, acts of extremist groups, 'skinheads' and 'National Fronts' in Brick Lane. I saw Brick Lane as a damp, dirty, dark, dull and degenerated place that attracted curb crawlers. From a 'slum' of darkness, neglect and squalor, I saw the hardworking Bangladeshi community, along with other communities, developing and leaving a hallmark of their contribution in creating a new, regenerated and vibrant Brick Lane – now known famously as the 'Curry Capital of Europe.

I saw our younger generation fought off extremists in mid-seventies and made brick lane a safer place to work, live and visit. I also witnessed the creations of famous buildings such as The Gherkin, The Shard, London Eye and Canary Wharf etc., not far from Brick Lane.

3

But Brick Lane has a distinctive identity of its own. What was once a 'Little France' is now a 'Little Sylhet'. What was once a 'voice for Whitechapel ghettos' is now a 'voice for Bangladeshi heroes'. What was once a cheap place has now become an expensive place. What was known as Whitechapel Lane once is now known as Brick Lane. However, it's not the game of name change that Brick Lane is famous for. It is famous for its cultural, social and economic identities, which have been transformed over generations.

Brick Lane is now a global visitor attraction. It has a Bengali pattern arch meant to show the merging of different cultures in this part of the world. Brick Lane played a big part during the liberation war of Bangladesh in 1971. Shahid Minar is a landmark in Altab Ali Park near Brick Lane.

The fight against racism started here in 1978. For the first time in history, a Bengali woman, Miss Rushanara Ali, was elected from this area as a member of the House of Commons. The first Executive Mayor of LBTH, Mr Lutfur Rahman, was elected in 2010 and re-elected in 2014 from this area too. A member of the House of Lords, Baroness Pola Manjila Uddin, also lived in Brick Lane and became involved in politics from there. The former British High

Commissioner to Bangladesh, His Excellency Mr Anwar Choudhury (currently serving as British Ambassador to Peru), received his childhood education from a school near Brick Lane.

Sapnara Khatun is the first Bangladeshi who holds the job of a senior judge in the British High Court since 2006 and has a strong connection with Brick Lane. Helal Abbas made history as a council leader of Tower Hamlets more than four times. Shirajul Haque Shiraj first introduced Boishakhi Mela from Brick Lane. Mesba Ahmed hit the headlines as the one and only Bangladeshi on the list of London's 1000 most influential people 2014, declared by The Evening Standard. He founded London Tigers, an initiative created to help change young people's lives through football, integration and social cohesion.

Dilara Khan and Nadia Ali launched the British-Bangladesh Chamber of Women Entrepreneurs from Brick Lane. Zakir Khan, Head of Community Affairs, Canary Wharf Group plc, made his mark from Brick Lane and combined the entire community and culture through his leadership. He became the Ambassador of West Ham United Football Club, which is such a prestigious post for a man of Bangladeshi origin.

All these famous names associated with Brick Lane are from Sylhet in Bangladesh.

Similarly, Syed Samadul Haque dreamt of his first Bangladeshi TV Channel 'Bangla TV' from Brick Lane. London Bangla Times started its first journey as 'online TV' from the Montefiore Centre. The first Boishakhi Mela, Pitha Utshob, Boi Mela and other cultural events originated from Brick Lane.

Glamour International was the first music centre, a video/audio and electronic shop opened in Brick Lane by the late Haji Moin Uddin Ahmed. Today, there are many similar businesses all over the country. Haji Moin Uddin's younger brother, Muquim Uddin Ahmed, also made money from Brick Lane. The first Bangladeshi employment bureau 'Shahnan' was opened in, and operated from, Brick Lane. Today, there are many employment centres across the country.

London Bangla Press Club started their journey from here and the headquarters of Sonali Bank is serving the community from this place. The historic London Jamme Mosque is in the heart of Brick Lane and London Muslim Centre (LMC) and East London Mosque are also a stone's throw from Brick Lane. Taj store has been in this street for nearly sixty years and a number of local travel agencies serving the community are among the oldest here.

The apex body of all trade organisations in UK, the British-Bangladesh Chamber of Commerce, is also on Greatorex St, off Brick lane. Greater Sylhet Development and Welfare Council are also close by. Ethnic Minority Enterprise Project (EMEP), with M A Rouf, Badrul Islam, Mosley Uddin, Abdul Haque Habib and others on board, helped the area to grow and prosper economically through restaurant training programmes. Mr Shah Munim and Osman Goni made their marks in the area through Brick Lane Housing and Community Trust.

Brick Lane is full of restaurants, mostly owned and managed by Bangladeshis. The restaurant owners are largely religious and most of them never sell alcohol because of their strong Islamic faith and beliefs. Brick Lane and many shop signs are written in Bengali and English, which one will not find elsewhere. There was a youth group formed by some formidable members of the Bangladeshi younger generation who were very active and vigilant and arranged marches and protests to force the BNP to remove their headquarters from Brick Lane.

For many such reasons, Brick Lane is in the heart of Bangladeshi community. Brick Lane, Britain, Banglatown and Bangladesh all are inseparable from each other.

I witnessed an act of terrorism and devastation in the Brick Lane nail bombing in 1997. Although my office was closed on the day the car bomb exploded, I visited the place the next day and saw the appalling aftermath. A few restaurants, including Sweet and Spice and Café Naz, took the full blast of the nail bomb; glasses were broken, windows were shattered and businesses were closed for several days.

I myself was the victim of a racist attack in 1976. I was assaulted by two thugs inside a tube station. The vicious attack damaged an organ and my right hip was operated on and fixed by a 'Richards Screw' in Mile End Hospital. I bear testimony to the skinheads who used to flock into Brick Lane, riding motorbikes to terrorise the locals and spread hatred within the neighbourhood. In the dead of night, these extremists used to throw stones at our windows. I received so many hate calls, even at night, but telephones will ring non-stop and when answered you hear nothing but swearing and verbal abuse.

We closed the shop early for safety reasons. Brick Lane, near Bethnal Green Road, was dark and only handful of shops were there, but everyone preferred to pull the shutters down when there were no customers. On Sundays, we closed the shop at 2pm. Dog Market used to be very busy on Sunday and Quaker Street and Cheshire Street were busy with footpath shops. Now, gentrification is taking place and only a few shops are seen near the Shoreditch side selling second-hand items from the footpath.

I was in Brick Lane when Altab Ali was murdered in 1978 and once lived in the same room in Reardon House, Reardon Street, Wapping as he did.

I have seen so much happen in Brick Lane, which is why I decided to write about it. This book is not like Monica Ali's Brick Lane, nor similar to Ansar Ullah or Phil Maxwell's books. This is about a home from home. It's about success stories of Bangladeshis. This is about a place that has always given me the nostalgic comfort of being at home in Bangladesh. In this book, I have tried to portray Brick Lane positively as a symbol of success, a place of inspiration, an area of motivation, an epicentre of many Bangladeshi activities, an epitome of many honourable works and an area with which one feels proud to be associated. I have tried to narrate the changes I witnessed throughout my attachment to the area for more than forty years.

I was always determined to write about the place I love and am obsessed about.

These are my personal memories; my own stories in my own words and my own experiences and personal views. I also tried to document the stories of other extraordinary Bangladeshis who are scattered from Aldgate to Polegate, Dockland to Scotland, Newham to Oldham, but wrote new chapters in places other than Brick Lane. They are the ones who still use Brick Lane as the nucleus of all their activities. I know for sure this is just a chapter, not a complete book. Many people have moved out of Brick Lane and are now enriching other places with their experiences from Brick Lane. Many of them are now teachers, journalists, community leaders, business leaders, business actors, investors, peacemakers, barristers, solicitors, doctors, caterers, judges, justices of peace, politicians, entrepreneurs, diplomats and philanthropists etc.

Mr Elash Miah Matin moved from Heanage Street, off of Brick Lane, to Milton Keynes. He established himself there and gave his children the best education. Moshahid bhai had a music centre called Zhonkar in Brick Lane. Thirty years ago he also left Brick Lane for Oldham and provided the best education to his children too. He is a renowned community leader. Mr

Atiqul Hoque, a former resident of Brick Lane, is now serving as a councillor on Salisbury City Council. Iqbal Ahmed OBE used to live around Brick Lane, but moved out to Cheshire where he has become a millionaire. Harun Miah, used to live near Brick Lane, but subsequently became a councillor and Deputy Mayor of Eastbourne. Mobarak Ali the owner of Brick Lane Music Centre also moved out, enriching his new area. There are hundreds of such remarkable stories of unsung heroes.

Brick Lane saw its first elected councillors, Barrister Ashik Ali and teacher Nurul Haque, in the London Borough of Tower Hamlets. Now we have councillors in many other places in the UK. Gulam Mortuja of Brick Lane was the first Bangladeshi Mayor in LBTH. Today, we have Mayors and Lord Deputy Mayors in Wales, Bath and other cities and towns. Abdul Mukit Chunu MBE is the first citizen of London Borough of Tower Hamlets. His attachment and contribution to Brick Lane is significant.

When most Asian restaurants were known as Indian restaurants, it was Abdus Salique who introduced his restaurant in Hanbury Street as a Bangladeshi Restaurant. In fact, the Dine Bangladesh campaign in1994 helped to change the nomenclature of Indian restaurants to Bangladeshi restaurants. As a result, Rajstani cuisine changed to Rajshahi cuisine. Star of India changed to Star of Bengal and Rose of India changed to Rose of Bengal etc. This very concept started to raise further awareness and enhanced the profile of Bangladesh.

The national profile was enhanced further when Bangladeshi restaurant Le Raj Avion became world's first flying restaurant in 1993. Le Raj of Epsom also made history by delivering Bangladeshi food and halal curry to the world's dignitaries in the Olympic and Paralympic Games in East End's Stratford in 2012.

The story of young Sabirul Islam is also very inspirational. He started his journey from Brick Lane to motivate one million youngsters in countries like Belgium, Brazil, Boston, Botswana and Bangladesh to become entrepreneurs. He was awarded 'Mosaic Entrepreneur of the Year' by HRH the Prince of Wales and Princess of Jordan. He received an international award from Japan and a CEO Award from Harvard Business School in the USA. He is also an author, editor, entrepreneur and a motivational global speaker.

Abdul Ali Jacko is a world kick boxing champion as well as a business leader, promoter, TV presenter and publisher. He became the first Asian to win the British, European and

Intercontinental Kickboxing Championship and brought name and fame for himself, his family and Brick Lane too.

In 2014, at the European Diversity Awards, Councillor Rabina Khan from Tower Hamlets Council won the prestigious 'Unilever Hero of the Year'. The European Diversity Awards recognise and celebrate those organisations and individuals that have shown innovation, creativity and commitment to equality, diversity and inclusion.

Also in 2014, Mr Ajmal Masroor was the only Bangladeshi whose name appeared in the annual list of 500 influential Muslims in the world, which also included the late King Abdullah of Saudi Arabia. Mr Masroor is a renowned TV Presenter, politician, author, fundraiser and Imam.

These are positive stories of Brick Lane vis-à-vis Bangladeshis.

This is the place proudly presenting and showcasing the positive achievements of Sylhetis in particular and Bangladeshis in general. Whether you are talking about culture or commerce, immigration or integration, fashion or finance, all these go together and Brick Lane is the place to be.

However, every coin has two sides and Brick Lane is no exception. I believe that the hustle and bustle of Brick Lane business might gradually disappear. Business in Brick Lane is now in the slow lane. Restaurants are hit by the recession, with staff shortages and reduced opening hours etc. Many businesses have already closed down, including sweat factories. Contemporary Café Naz, Dawat, Shalimar, Sweet and Spice, Bangla City, Clifton and many more have closed down. Dawat Indian restaurant has changed hands to Moo restaurant; Sweet and Spicy restaurant changed to Caffe Kimbo; Café Naz Express to Money Exchange; Modern Saree Centre to Cakes and Gateau; Shiraz to Shaad; Clifton to Efes Turkish restaurant and Le Taj to an Italian restaurant. Many businesses are struggling to survive.

Social mobility is causing Bangladeshis to move out further east because of a dramatic rise in property prices in the area and because of its close proximity to two powerful places. Brick Lane herself is a neighbour of commercial and political powers. The City of London is a seat of commercial power and the City of Westminster is a seat of political power. A more affluent community is coming in and slowly taking over. There is already a £1,000,000 residential property on Princelet Street, opposite my office, which has been purchased by a non-Bangladeshi from a Bangladeshi freeholder. A wealthy millionaire recently purchased a property on Fournier Street, off Brick Lane.

This is the story of transformations and changes taking place in Brick Lane. Communities are arriving one after the other. Before the Muslim Bangladeshi community, it was predominantly a European Jewish community. Before that, it was the Irish and French Huguenot weavers' community. Jews have now moved out to North London in places like Hendon, Golders Green, Kilburn, Cricklewood, Bushey and Stamford Hill. The Irish moved out to the Hampstead and Dagenham areas. Similarly, many Bangladeshis are either renting out their properties or buying second homes and making their eastern move to places like Newham, Barking, Redbridge, Ilford, Romford, Chadwell Heath, Gants Hill, Upney, Upminster and becoming detached from Brick lane.

The truth is that communities may not be sustained in one place due to regeneration, but the glory of Brick Lane's Bangladeshi community will always remain embedded in history. It is a fact that Brick Lane helped to build up places like Bank, Bloomsbury and Belgravia etc. when the Great Fire of London in 1666 gutted these places. Bricks used to be transported through Brick Lane by horse drawn delivery carts to build those areas; hence the name 'Brick' Lane.

However, the Brick Lane of yesterday is not the same Brick Lane of today. It has changed enormously and it will change a lot tomorrow. It has endured tough times. However, some of my memories of Brick Lane are still clear, but before they fade away, I have tried to pen them in this book. For obvious reasons, it is not unusual to make errors, so I hope the readers will excuse my inadvertent mistakes, will look at the decades of changes around the area and will judge for themselves on the merit of a book written by an 'amateur first time writer' like myself. I might have lost a lot of my old memories because of my old age, diabetes, glaucoma, CHD and other medical conditions, but I have tried to complete the book with passion, perseverance and patience. It's not about perfection though and has been written in my own simple words, style and vocabulary.

I did, however, seek help and suggestions from my family and expert friends. My only brother, Brigadier General (Rtd) Humayun Bakth Muhit, assisted me with his professional advice and suggested that I publish a translated book in Bengali. My youngest son Zayn, Safwan and daughter Eva who is busy in her profession as pharmacy purchasing technician, helped me with their computer knowledge. My wife Sherina and my daughter-in-law Maisha encouraged me to carry on writing the book. Thanks to Maisha for designing the book cover, although as a new mum she is busy with her child Isla. Shahnan, my eldest son, busy in his new appointment as Senior Vice President of Deutsch Bank, found time to offer ideas and suggested the title for the book. Bashir Ahmed, Mohib Choudhury, Osman Goni, Dilara Khan, Taysir Mahmud, Abul Hayat Nurujjaman and Shahida Rahman helped me with their advice and suggestions. His Excellency Dr A K Abdul Momen, Mr Enam Ali, MBE, FIH, Anne Main MP, Dr Abul Kalam Azad, Dr Sean Carey and Baroness Pola Uddin went through the manuscripts and gave their valuable comments and reviews. I am grateful to Professor John Eade for taking his time and writing the preface for the book.

I only hope this book is used as a future reference. One day the future generation might eagerly seek information about their ancestors and their forefathers who once lived and worked and had connections with Brick Lane. They might find some answers, information, stories and comfort from this book.

It would be a wonderful resource for schools and would help young people (from all cultures) to develop greater respect and understanding of different communities. After all, we all belong to the same race - the human race!

'From Thousand Miles to Thousand Smiles'

The year was 1973, the month September; the exact date forgotten. A British Overseas Airways Corporation (now British Airways or BA) aircraft was preparing to take off from Kurmitola Airport, Dacca (now Dhaka) for Doha, en route to London Heathrow. I was so excited and was looking forward to the journey on this DC-10 jet. Happiness turned to sadness when the time came to say goodbye to my brother Mumit, maternal Uncle Nazrul Islam and other relatives who came to see me off at Tejgaon Airport. I had already said farewell to my parents, family members and friends before departing from Sunamganj and Sylhet. After finishing all the immigration formalities, checking in and saying my goodbyes, I settled down to relax in the airport lounge with only one piece of hand luggage with me.

Many thoughts occupied my mind. After all, I was leaving my homeland, my near and dear ones and was uncertain when I would return, or whether I would find my relatives alive or dead. I suddenly realised that I had some left over takas (Bangladesh currency) in my pocket, which were of no use in the country of my destination.

Immediately, I decided to empty my pocket and give it to my brother Mumit, because he loved to go shopping. I thought he must have been waiting on the open top floor of the airport from where everyone could wave off their relatives. However, I could not go out, since the immigration formalities and security checks had already been completed. I approached an officer and asked whether I could pop out for a while. He kindly gave permission. I hurried up the stairs to the open top floor to look for my brother. I spotted him right in the front row leaning against the wall to catch a good glimpse of me while boarding the aircraft. I called his name and he looked back, surprised to see me again. I gave him the left over takas and told him to do his shopping in Dhaka before going back to Sunamganj. He was so happy. I embraced him once again and made my way back to the lounge before boarding the plane.

When the announcement was made, the passengers queued up on the tarmac leading to the aircraft steps. At this point, I had another chance to look back and see my relatives again. My eyes locked with my brother's. I waved until I reached the top of the steps and paused for a moment before giving a final wave. In those days, Dhaka did not have a jet bridge for its passengers to transfer from terminals to aeroplanes.

I boarded the aircraft, found my window seat, fastened the seat belt tried to look for my relatives through the window.

I had no money at all; my pocket was empty. However, I knew that my sponsor, the late Akhlakur Rahman Choudhury, would be waiting for me at the airport with others and that I should have no problem for money whatsoever. It was a good flight and the plane landed at Doha at midnight local time. After refuelling, it took off again for London.

After nearly seven long hours the plane landed safely at London Heathrow Airport. All the way, from the runway to the waiting queue, I looked around, eagerly exploring the new place. I noticed that the people looked happy and were smiling, not depressed or sad looking at all. I smiled at the immigration lady to whom I handed my passport for checking. She returned my smile and on that first day I fell in love with the people and the country.

Following immigration formalities and collecting my luggage from the belt, I found the exit and saw Sayeek, Subash and others waiting for me. I was greeted and embraced and was so pleased to see my relatives. They gave me a hand in pushing the trolley and took me to a restaurant nearby. They entertained me first with tea and biscuits before we dashed off by car. I was staring at the street lights and could not remember when I fell asleep.

The next morning, some visitors came to see me. First there was Shahida Mina and her husband. They are from my home town Sunamganj and were eager to meet me. They talked about the current issues in Bangladesh and enquired about our home town and the newly created country. Many had not visited their motherland for many years. In those days it was not easy to communicate with friends and relatives as we do today instantly through the internet and social media. After a long chat, they stood up to leave, but before they did so they gave me few pounds in cash and a shirt as a gift. I was very embarrassed and hesitated in accepting the gifts. I was not used to receiving gifts like that and really felt awkward, but I had to accept with gratitude so as not to offend them.

The next person to visit was someone from the local neighbourhood not known to me at all. They did exactly the same. They wanted to know the latest news of the country and our district. Before leaving, they left a gift for me.

My college classmate Awlad, who came to London before me for higher education, found out about my arrival and came over to say hello to me. Before saying goodbye, he also handed over a five pound note and said, 'Just take it and never refuse. Refusal will offend.'

Since then, I never refused and rather started to expect cash gifts from both known and unknown people. As a result, within a few days I had quite a lot of cash in my pocket from friends and strangers. I was later briefed that this has become a tradition, a culture within our community, to help out and support a new arrival with a sort of start-up finance. What a great idea, which still exists in our close-knit community. I don't know of anywhere else in the world that practices this superb idea. Now I follow the same rules I learnt from my older generation. Whenever a new guest comes to the UK, my gift takes the same shape; the British pound. This practice is still ongoing. I think this tradition is meaningful, because it helps and supports a newcomer with a cash fund. It teaches you how to be supportive to others. It teaches humanity, brotherhood, bonding, love, respect, solidarity and a sense of togetherness. That is community spirit. That is in a way similar to the government's unemployment benefit.

The community had bad practices too. They used to buy expensive gifts for visiting politicians and tourists from Bangladesh, but they soon found out that they don't reciprocate. Now that practice has ceased to some extent in last decade, which is good news. Moreover, the people coming from other side are wealthier now than most of the hardworking people living on this side. However, the 'small cash gift' phenomenon continues.

From the moment I arrived until today, I have certainly worked hard, earned money, gained experience and learnt many things about the UK and am in a better position to express my own judgement on the place, its people, its politics and its principles.

I can now loudly and proudly say that Britain is one of the best countries in the world in which to live. British people are the best people in the world to integrate with and British values and principles are the best in the world to share, practice and preach. Apart from money and wealth, these are my ultimate assets that I can live with happily and pass over to my next generation, so that they live their lives happily too. I would like to treasure these as valuable achievements of my entire life.

Other achievements include my happy family and happy children, who were born, raised and received an excellent education and the best upbringing here. I earned respect in the community, have my own business, a decent house, a decent car and a decent family etc.

I was honoured to be nominated as an official parliamentary candidate for the Conservative Party twice. It was amazing to receive the historic 'Freedom of the City of London' and an accolade of 'Community Champion' by Canary Wharf Group. It was an honour also to be invited to the Buckingham Palace Garden Party, which I attended twice with my wife Sherina. I was also invited by the former British Prime Minister Sir John Major and his wife Norma Major to 10 Downing Street and enjoyed the time at the Prime Minister's official residence with my wife. In October 2014, it was again a privilege to celebrate Eid with the Prime Minister, the Rt Hon David Cameron at10 Downing Street, along with many community leaders.

I served as President of the British-Bangladesh Chamber of Commerce. It was indeed an Honour to be at the helm of this apex body of all Bangladeshi trade organisations in UK and had the opportunity to lead two trade missions; one to Bangladesh and the other to the United Nations. I had the honour of meeting with the present Bangladesh Prime Minister, the Rt Hon Sheikh Hasina and the former Prime Minister, Rt Hon Khaleda Zia in their official residence. In the UN, we had series of meetings with high profile dignitaries such as the Deputy Secretary General of the UN and numerous ambassadors, including my classmate Dr A K Abdul Momen, the permanent representative of Bangladesh in the UN. I am privileged to serve as a judge on the British Curry Awards, which is a world platform for caterers and known as the Curry Oscar of the Industry. I am also honoured to have served four times as a Chief Election Commissioner for a renowned Bangladeshi community organisation called Greater Sylhet Development and Welfare Council, UK, as well as acting as a Chief Election Commissioner for the Bangladesh Caterers Association UK (BCA). I feel honoured to see my name engraved on the Millennium Bridge, opened by Her Majesty the Queen. I was privileged to be present on the first day of the opening of this historic bridge. What else do I expect? There was an extraordinary knowledge gap for me, which I have managed to fill to some extent.

When I reflect back, I remember the day when I embarked on a life journey with nothing in my pocket. Now I have everything. This country is now my own country. It is my home and my children's home. It's a home from home. This nation has given me everything in abundance. I do not want to measure these achievements and success by the material things. I have earned something else for my future generations, which cannot be measured with a scale, nor can you put a price on its value. These include Britishness, happiness, safety, security, stability, healthcare, wellbeing, respect, opportunities, democracy and tolerance etc. These are the positive things I have accomplished, which place me in a comfort zone.

This is only my own story. I know hundreds of Bangladeshis out there with similar, different or even better and brighter stories who also had nothing, but now have more than I do. They are certainly contributing significantly to British society and the British economy too. Many of them have been awarded an MBE or OBE from Her Majesty the Queen as recognition for their good works. Their story is our community's story. Their success is our community's success. It's all because of their hard work, dedication, devotion and determination.

The following quote is certainly true: 'Coming together is the beginning. Keeping together is a progress. Working together is a success'. The first generation of Bangladeshis came together, then kept together, worked together in factories and restaurants and achieved success together.

I am thankful and grateful to Britain. They welcomed us as a guest community and gave us equal opportunities, just like any other citizen. There is no difference and no disparity. That's why I would like to show my gratitude to this great country, the Great Britain. I remember a quote from Roman Philosopher Cicero, who said, 'Let us rise up and be thankful, for gratitude is not only the greatest virtues, but the parent of all virtues'.

Work, Women and Weather

You should not always rely on three w's in the UK, they say. You could be hired and fired from your work place at any time. I was wondering how it could be possible in a civilised world. When I was working in Bangladesh, I never even dreamt of getting sacked. But here I have to be very careful and very loyal to my boss, otherwise I will be at risk of losing my job. Just like the unpredictable British weather, people frequently change their jobs. I even heard that women change their boyfriends quite often! Anyway, I was not worried about the weather or women; I was more concerned about finding a stable job that would give me joy and stability.

So, one chilly morning in 1974, I started looking for a job. It began with a journey on the district line train and alighting at Stepney Green tube station. It was snowing heavily and Mile End Road appeared whiter than white. It looked lovely, especially for me, as I had arrived in Britain only a year previously and had never seen such white snow before. It really was a fantastic sight. I enjoyed the sight of huge soft flakes drifting down from the sky. However, it was too cold and I thought I was freezing to death. I was not used to such cold weather because I came from a hot country. I started to walk as fast as possible to keep myself warm. I was desperate to get an official job. I didn't worry about the wages. I was walking fast; my hopes were rising and I soon arrived at the door of Crimson Enterprise, Mile End Road, where Dhaka Biriani now stands.

The late Haji Moin Uddin Ahmed and Mr Abed Khan were both partners of this newly opened travel agency and cargo business. I knew Mr Abed Khan as I was a Sunamganj correspondent of his daily English newspaper 'The People'. The late Haji Moin Uddin Ahmed was even more acquainted with me and my family from Sylhet. Haji Moin Uddin was a very prominent, smart and humble businessman. He owned a travel and tourism business in Sylhet and in London that was his first new business venture. The office looked very modern and the layout was excellent. They conducted my interview, which went well and I was offered the job.

In those days, there were not many official jobs available in East End of London. The area had a lot of opportunities for those who wanted to work in the rag trade. The new job gave me a ray of hope, aspiration and satisfaction. The wage was very low, but there was no minimum wage in those days. Nevertheless, I was happy to have a job in an office, a place to live upstairs and a team of good colleagues. I became a regular customer at the nearby Restaurant 'India Grill'; my lunch only cost 50p and included rice, curry, a papadum and salad.

In 1975, Moin bhai bought a freehold shop at 48 Brick Lane. He had to spend some money on it before using it as an office cum residence, so he employed builders to renovate it. This later became my workplace with an adjacent living room and from where I became familiar with Brick Lane. This was the place where I could see the Bangladeshi people walking up and down the road, doing their shopping, queuing for cinema next door and meeting and chatting with each other. However, it was not a good place for working or living, even in the standard of those days. People who lived outside the Brick Lane area considered themselves to be of a better class. They looked down at those who lived and worked in Brick Lane. Even my friends did not like me working there, because they said I didn't fit the area. The noise from cinema hall penetrated the wall and I could hear the dialogues and songs of the films being shown next door. The noise disturbed my sleep too, but I became used to it.

Nirala, Naz and Nail Bomb

My workplace and residence soon became a commercial hub and a meeting point for working class Bangladeshis. The first Bangladeshi music centre 'Glamour International' became a popular shop where there was no language barrier and Bengali customers could purchase everything from electronics goods to gift items for their beloved relatives before travelling to Bangladesh. They even had the opportunity to buy their travel tickets and send personal effects by sea or air cargo from the company's subsidy wing, Milfa Travels.

Muquim Ahmed and I lived upstairs at 48 Brick Lane in two small separate rooms. In the daytime it was busy with customers, but in the evening it was silent, dark and boring, with nowhere to go. The small black and white TV was not sufficient for passing time. There were no Bangladeshi TV channels or Bangladeshi radio stations like Betar Bangla, Spectrum or the BBC Asian Network. So, most of the evenings we used to spend recording music on cassettes – C-60, C-90 and C120 – or watching Indian films on videos. Today, we hardly see the use of cassettes or videos. These have been replaced by YouTube, CDs, DVD's, USB pen drives, computers, the internet, WhatsApp and social networking sites such as Twitter and Facebook. In those days, people not only used to listen to music on cassettes, but on LP or SP records. In fact, Milfa Ltd was the first to make LP and SP recordings of Himangshu Goswami, Kari Amir Uddin and Shefali Ghosh. The days of record and cassette players have long gone. Mono was replaced by stereo. Now you can download millions of songs from the internet or YouTube. In the past, it was hard to find a song of your own choice. Now you can easily Google it and record any song from any year in any language and save it as a 'favourite'.

Life is much easier now than before. Commodities are also cheaper than before. With scientific advancement and development came changes. People stopped going out and watching movies in cinemas. They could comfortably watch videos in their home environment. They could pause, stop, rewind or fast forward at their own will. This is how 'Naz Cinema' became a casualty and slowly started to lose customers, eventually having to close down.

When people started to benefit from YouTube, Google or the internet, video shops started to lose their businesses. Music centres that once dominated the market began to close down. Brick Lane lost shops like Glamour International, Shahnan Showbiz, Zhankar, Modern Music Centre, Meera, JR etc. Glamour and Milfa both disappeared, but were resurrected as Café Naz – a brand name in catering. Café Naz Express, Café Naz Corvino and Café Naz in Brick Lane all closed down unfortunately. Café Naz was a landmark in Brick Lane. It used to be Mayfair Cinema, which turned into Naz Cinema. Part of Naz became a music centre, then transformed into an upmarket restaurant, which unfortunately closed down too. Café Naz took the full blast of the nail bomb in 1997, but it survived. Skinheads have gone. The new EDL and BNP could not enter into Brick Lane. The supermarket 'Bangla City' closed down in January 2014. Brick Lane survived racism, so hopefully it will survive the recession too.

In the mid-70s, Nirala was a small coffee bar with a big name within the Bangladeshi community in Brick Lane. It was opposite the Naz Cinema where the Al-Badar Fried Chicken and Curry Restaurant now stands. Bangladeshi restaurant workers and cinema goers were the regular customers of this restaurant, whereas Clifton Restaurant – farthest from Nirala – was another hub for mainly Pakistani and mainstream customers. The Kray Twins were good customers at Clifton. When Clifton's owner, Musa Patel, died, it was taken over by a Bangladeshi businessman, Mr Azmal, and changed its name to Preem Restaurant.

Azmal Hussain, owner of Preem Restaurant in Brick Lane

Workers from outside London used to use Nirala as a commercial hub in Brick Lane. Before the start of a movie at the cinema across the road, or after the end of the movie, people used to crowd into this small café bar to enjoy good company, food and soft drinks. In those days, there were more Bangladeshi men than women and Nirala Restaurant catered for single men. Those who remember the famous Modhur Café in Dhaka University can somehow compare this to Nirala Café. Both cafés attracted students as well as politicians. The only difference is that Modhur Café is still there, while Nirala is not. It was transformed into a video shop before changing again into its present state of a fast food shop. Sadly, its image and uniqueness are gone.

People's lives are too fast; they do not sit for long, waste time or gossip anymore, especially in their lunch hour. It reminds me of the famous song by Manna Dey: 'Coffee house er shei adda ta ar nei'. When translated, it means: 'Those days are gone when friends used to enjoy their time together over coffee'. Indeed, in those days, people used to gossip over a cup of tea and made the restaurant a meeting point in Brick Lane, before dispersing to watch Hindi or Bengali movies in Naz Cinema, or sending money to their relatives back home in Bangladesh. Even those who did not have a permanent address to provide to a doctor's surgery to obtain a medical card, used Nirala's address and were helped out.

The renowned Bangladeshi actor/director Khan Ataur Rahman also used to visit this restaurant quite often. The Nirala not only served food, but catered for the different needs of the community as well. People had nowhere to go; there were no clubs, community centres or offices of any community organisations you see today, so they used places like Nirala and Milfa to meet. They spent a little money on tea and samosas and spent a great deal of their free time gossiping or discussing the country of their origin before visiting their relatives in Tower Hamlets or Newham.

Naz and Nirala both had common customers and were right opposite each other. However, from both Naz and Nirala, a third party benefited most: Glamour International. Glamour International was a popular shop, a first port of call for Bangladeshis doing their 'home visit' shopping. Glamour International, next door to Naz Cinema Hall, used to sell products needed for use in Bangladesh's rural areas. Items like torches, lighters, tape recorders, transistor radios, gift items, Seiko 5 watches, music players, cassettes, electronic items and batteries etc. were in great demand. Customers had a great passion for spending money on items for their nearest and dearest.

Glamour International was the only Bangladeshi retail shop, apart from Chopra, Sami and Salim and Houndsditch Warehouse etc. They could also buy their air tickets and send money or personal effects by air or sea cargo from Glamour International. They could manage everything under one roof and within their budget. Glamour International was an affordable shop for working Bangladeshi customers. It was definitely a hugely popular, incredibly reliable, affordable and adorable shopping outlet for the community of yesteryear.

Place, People and Politics

Brick Lane was not a hub for politics in the past. Members of the Bangladeshi community used to converge in Brick Lane for social gatherings, community shopping, annual Eid prayers or attending funerals in mosques. But as the family grew, the community became better off economically and they decided to buy residential properties, with many moving out of Brick Lane. I remember attending a funeral in East London Mosque in 1977. Only a handful of worshippers were present. Today, at any funeral, in any mosque, it is full of worshippers.

Bangladeshis are now seen in every town and every city in the UK. They have their own mosques, community schools, community centres, community organisations and so on. However, politics unites them to come to Brick Lane. They hire buses and coaches from far away to get together near Brick Lane, particularly in Altab Ali Park. Shahid Minar becomes a meeting point from where they start their procession to take their demands to 10 Downing Street, or march towards Trafalgar Square.

Brick Lane becomes a focal point for Bangladeshi politics. Politics not only unites, but sometimes divides the community too.

When two opposing political parties meet at Altab Ali Park, they sometimes become confrontational and British police have to intervene and disperse the crowd. Because Bangladesh is polarised over politics, the Bangladeshi community in Brick Lane is also divided. You rarely see opposing party members sitting down at the same table in the same restaurant and debating Bangladesh politics. On the other hand, you can see different political parties giving business mainly to those restaurants who support them. Even a mosque committee is sometimes found to be sympathetic to certain political parties. Furthermore, British election results could be tilted by the support of any identified mosques in some cases.

While Bangladeshi politics centre round Altab Ali Park, British politics centre round mosques, particularly in LBTH. When I was twice a candidate in parliamentary elections, I noticed a particular mosque supporting a particular candidate in both elections in 2001 and in 2005. As a Conservative candidate, fighting an election was a thrilling experience for me in LBTH. Politics is nothing without community involvement. Since I was involved with the community for such a long period of time, I decided to stand, participate, contribute and become engaged in elections.

If Brick Lane did not cultivate the political field, we would probably not see a Bangladeshi MP in Westminster today. I know many people in LBTH who are interested in politics. They worked very hard and invested a lot of their time and effort in local and mainstream politics. Peter Gold, Zakir Khan, Subrina Hossain, ASH Zaman, David Fell, Ataur Rahman Ata, Dr Anwara Ali, Shafi Choudhury, Sweb Choudhury Faisal, Richard Holden, Paul Ingham, Mohammed Nazimuddin, Stephanie Smith, Belal Ahmed, Rajon Uddin Jalal, Baroness Pola Uddin, Ohid Ahmed, Simon Gordon Clerk, Syed Mizan, Nurul Haque, Dinah Glover, Tony Glover, Gulam Mortuja, Claire Palmer, Mr Akikur Rahman, Ashok Ali, Helal Abbas, Janet Ludlow, Helal Rahman, Kumar Murshed, Neil King, Syed Nurul Islam Dulu, Oona King, Ajmol Masroor, Abzol Miah, Mina Rahman, Shofik Ahmed, Jewel Islam, Doros Ullah, John Biggs, Mahbub Alam, Shahed Ali, Shah Alam, Khales Uddin, Haroon Miah, Shiria Khatun, Matinuzzaman, Matt Smith, Syed Hussain Ahmed, Attic Rahman, Abdul Mojid, Fazal Uddin, Abdal Ullah, Abdus Sukur, Sajjad Miah, Abdul Matin, Jane Emmerson, Tim Archer, SM Azam, Abdul

Asad, Ahmed Hussain, Edna Hill, Sheikh Eaor, David Webb, Jamal Khan, Chris Wilford, George Galloway, Cllr Md Ayas Miah, Maium Miah, Muquim Ahmed, Oliur Rahman, Gulam Robbani, Ansar Mustaquim, Rajib Ahmed, Suluk Ahmed, Somshul Haque, Peter Shore, Shirajul Islam, Denise Jones, Aminur Khan, Jan Alam, Rois Ali and many others from different political parties worked hard, sacrificed their time and made contributions to local and national politics.

Since 1997, until the last parliamentary election, it was only the Conservative Party who elected their official candidates to stand for Bethnal Green and Bow constituency, who happened to be Bangladeshis. In the last parliamentary election, after Zakir Khan, it was Matthew Smith who stood as a Conservative candidate. In 2005 and 2001, the prospective parliamentary candidate was S B Faruk. In 1997, Dr Kabir Choudhury fought this seat as a Conservative candidate. He later changed sides and supported George Galloway in his political campaign in Sylhet. The political cultivation began around 2001, but only in 2010 was Bangladeshi Rushanara Ali MP elected as a labour candidate. In the mayoral election, Mr Lutfur Rahman fought his way through to become elected as an independent candidate and made history as the first Executive Mayor of LBTH in 2010. On 22 May 2014, he was re-elected as a candidate for Tower Hamlets.

Again, it is Brick Lane and its voters who play an important role and are a deciding factor in any election, be it a council election, mayoral election, European or parliamentary election. Directly or indirectly, I think Brick Lane plays a vital part in both Bangladeshi and British politics. Community politics in inner cities are different to those in suburbia. The election hubbub never dies down in Brick Lane. BBC Panorama, East End Newspapers, TV and LBC etc., make the election news in LBTH the talk of the moment.

Renowned Bangladeshi writers like Abdul Gaffar Choudhury and BBC reporter Andrew Gilligan reported Mayor Lutfur's election result, influenced by the supporters of extremists and Islamic radicalists, while Richard Symoor of the Guardian and Asok Kumar commented positively on Lutfur's election victory. Again, it was mainly his opponents from Brick Lane who filed a case against Lutfur Rahman on alleged vote rigging. Community Minister Eric Pickles ordered an investigation. Petitions were submitted to the police for investigation into the promise of houses for votes and illegal tactics to win the mayoral election in May 2014. They branded his main rival (labour candidate, John Biggs) as racist and anti-Islamic, with allegations of widespread voting fraud, doctoring of ballot papers, manipulation of postal voting, and sabotage of his rival's chances.

The petition against Mr Lutfur Rahman was submitted by residents Azmal Hussain, Andrew Eriam and Angela Moffat. The bombshell allegation report and key findings were published in the Evening Standard on 4 November 2014. The PwC auditors' report slammed the council for flouting spending rules over millions of pounds worth of grants and property sales. Eventually, Lutfur Rahman was found guilty of corruption and illegal practices and was banned from standing again. The long-awaited verdict came on 23 April 2015. The mayoral election was again held on 11 June 2015. John Biggs, the labour candidate, defeated independent candidate Rabina Khan and was elected as a new mayor of Tower Hamlets.

In other developments, in other places in London, we saw the election victory of two Bangladeshi women – Rupa Huq and Tulip Siddiq – who were elected MPs in the British Parliament in May 2015.

To be a prospective parliamentary candidate for the Conservative Party is not that easy. You have to go through a robust process. When I became a PPC from Bethnal Green and Bow constituency, I had to follow the same procedure; you have to be the member of the party first and you have to apply for the nomination. The local association will scrutinise the applications before shortlisting.

In 2001, there were 33 applicants interested in standing for Bethnal Green and Bow. It was shortlisted down to seven. They were interviewed by the association selection committee. Three were selected from the shortlist, including myself, and we were then interviewed by the central office before going to Milton Keynes for a full day's interview and written test. The written test was much harder than the Bangladesh Civil Service written exam. I sat such an exam and found too difficult. Within a certain time frame, you have to provide your answers. In the group discussion, you are watched by two examiners before they mark you. You then have a face-to-face interview with a sitting MP. He asks you to choose one of three topics on which to give five-minute talk. After this, the MP will signpost you for your next task. When everything is over, you are informed of your exam result by post.

Within two weeks, I received my result over post. I did not tell my family about the exam, just in case. However, when I opened the envelope and read the positive result, I broke the good news to my wife. I was overwhelmed. Half the battle was won. That's not the end. I had to come back to face the final hustings with members. Three finalists were competing and we had to deliver a five-minute speech, followed by a Q&A session. Members from the floor had their chance to ask questions and three judges were there to decide the fate of candidates. After the hustings we were told to wait in a separate room. The judges had their time to mark and make their minds up.

They sent someone downstairs to call me up and congratulated me on being the new PPC. The other candidates were congratulated too. At the end, I had to deliver my speech. I thanked the voters for selecting me as their prospective parliamentary candidate. I congratulated the other candidates and praised them too. In my speech, I mentioned that Conservative values are those of Bangladeshi values. We respect our elders, we strongly believe in family values and we believe in working hard and looking after family members. Our community believes in entrepreneurship, business and creating jobs. The money we make supports not just an individual, but the entire family. I find Conservative values are similar to mine. They have high regard and respect for Her Majesty the Queen. They reward hardworking people and do not like people being on the dole.

In 2001, the parliamentary selection process of Bethnal Green and Bow constituency took place at the upstairs of a pub Black Lion. This is now closed down. In 2005 the process took place in Montefiori Centre in Hanbury Street.

Bethnal Green and Bow constituency used to be known as Bethnal Green and Stepney constituency. The boundary has changed since. Poplar and Lime House is now known as Poplar and Canning Town constituency.

Rushanara Ali MP addressing a meeting of BBCC

Labour Party election campaign in Tower Hamlets

Conservative Muslim Forum

Associations, Awards and Accolades

Spectacular Award Night

The Bangladeshi community in Great Britain stretches from Aldgate to Polegate and from Dockland to Scotland. This community was never a dormant community. Wherever they settled, they wanted to make it a close knit community. They believed in forming associations to become acquainted with each other, to work together for the welfare of each other, to develop the community together, to speak for themselves and others and to remain together as an active community. Most of these 'value-driven' associations are motivated by the desire to achieve social or commercial goals and public welfare.

Even before the independence of Bangladesh, the community formed an association in the UK called East Pakistan Welfare Association, which became known as Bangladesh Welfare Association and was actively supportive to the community with its office at 39 Fournier Street, next door to Brick Lane Jamme Mosque. Unfortunately, this ceased to function but the same name is now being used in other places in Croydon, Tunbridge Wells and Enfield etc.

Bangladesh Caterers Association (BCA) is the oldest organisation, relentlessly working for the development of this growing catering industry since 1960. Until now, it has been representing restaurants in their thousands, lobbying to the British law makers to look after the best interests of the industry and holding spectacular annual gala dinners in prestigious premises, making it a memorable event for its members and guests. Israel Miah was the first Chairman of this catering association, while the present Chairman is Pasha Khandaker. The current Secretary is M A Munim and Chief Treasurer is Abdul Malik. I was honoured to serve once as its Chief Election Commissioner. Although their HQ is in Harrow, Middlesex, they have a good connection and a lot of members from the Brick Lane area.

Brick Lane itself has seen the birth of many Bangladeshi community organisations, such as Brick Lane Business Association, Brick Lane Restaurant Association, Traders Association, Brick Lane Illumination Association, UKBATA, East London Small Business Centre, Sunamganj Probashi Shomity (SUPROBASH), Spitalfields Small Business Association (SsBA), Spitalfields Housing Association, Sylhet Sadar Association and many more.

The newly established British-Bangladesh Caterers Association (BBCA) began their spectacular journey on 10 June 2015 from the East End of London. In the presence of chief guest, The Rt Hon Nicky Morgan MP (Education Secretary), the new President Yafor Ali, Secretary Shahanoor Khan, Treasurer Elais Miah Motin and other leaders vowed to play an

51

important role in advancing the curry industry, creating opportunities for employment, skill and training and making the industry stronger from length and breadth of the UK.

BBCC is the apex body of all Bangladeshi trade organisations in Great Britain. It is in the heartland of the Bangladeshi community and since 1993 has built its track record, driven by skilled professionals, and has an excellent organisational structure.

BBCC is an important driving force in the business community. It has its leadership, the experience, goodwill, confidence, resources and networks. It has ongoing programmes to add to its members' knowledge and experience so that they become business experts in their respective commercial fields.

It has successfully delivered a number of projects for the benefit of the business community. It has opened up four chapters in

Greece, France, Holland and Italy. BBCC took high profile delegates to Bangladesh and the United Nations too. They organised a single country Expo in London and recently opened new chapters in different regions within the UK.

The founder President of BBCC was the late M A Rahim and the present President is Mr Mahtab Choudhury. Its Director General is Mohib Choudhury, while Finance Director is Sydur Rahman Renu. I was fortunate to be at its helm for one term and felt honoured to serve this great organisation as its President.

GSC has their head office at 135 Commercial Street, off Brick Lane. This is the only charity organisation formed by the initiatives of Sylheti community that serves the interest of all the communities in general. They have been engaged in supporting community development and social welfare for nearly twenty years. They have a branch in Bangladesh too and look after the community at home and abroad. They have a huge network, a decent membership list and an excellent record of community work. They have successfully connected communities from north to south and east to west. Their 'drop-in' advice service in Aldgate is testament to their willingness and openness to remain close to the community and serve them to the best of their ability. Their former President was barrister Ataur Rahman and the present President is Nurul Islam Mahbub. Ashab Beg has been replaced by Syed A Q Kaiser as Secretary and Firuj Khan is the treasurer. I was privileged to conduct a few annual elections as their Chief Election Commissioner.

Greater Sylhet Development Council (GSC)

London Bangla Press Club is so prestigious that when invited to join them as a life member in 2005, I agreed without a second thought. I probably paid their £2,000 membership fee immediately! They have professional and renowned journalists in their team and many community leaders and businessmen joined them as life members because of the involvement of highly professional editors, reporters, correspondents and journalists. I felt honoured to be invited as an observer in their elections twice. I have always high regard and respect for those who are associated with print and electronic media.

I remember that the late Dr Bashir Ahmed, Founder of the Surma Newsweekly, came to 48 Brick Lane in 1978 and we kept a few copies of the first edition of Surma on our shop shelf for sale, or just to give away. I was probably the first person to take a copy of this paper and read it. Since then, I have never forgotten Bashir sahib or his paper.

On another recent occasion, while delivering a project of UKTI as BBCC President, I decided to organise a workshop for journalists. I felt that with the advancement of modern technology, we now live in a media-saturated environment, so any workshop on media would be fine. I contacted my colleague Mr Ahmed us Samad

Chowdhury and with his help I hired a speaker from Channel S and arranged the workshop in our BBCC committee room at Greatorex Street. The young speaker, Tauhid Shakil, who happened to be their newsreader, started his speech by saying that 'NEWS' means information coming from North, East, West and South. We all liked his introductory speech, enjoyed the entire programme and were satisfied with the journalist speakers, which later helped us to secure further funding for delivering other projects successfully.

I believe that because of London Bangla Press Club, The British Association of Journalists and other similar organisations, the Bangladeshi community is now very much an informed community. In 1975, Janomot was the only Bangladeshi newspaper sold from our shop at 48 Brick Lane, followed by Surma Newsweekly. Now the number of print newspapers is increasing significantly. Around fourteen different Bengali newspapers are now available in the market. However, electronic media is speedily taking over. The total number of Bangladeshi TV channels currently stands at six. The breaking news is transmitted instantly, whereas we have to wait a week to get a printed paper in our hand. Whether it is print or electronic media, a press club or journalists' association, it is the community that is benefitting from all of them.

TV channels used to charge annual fees in the past, but now it's free. Bangladeshi TV channel NTV Europe took part in the Asian Viewers Television Awards and won the prize in October 2015 by defeating Indian Bengali channel Star Jalsha and others. Nowadays, some newspapers are moderately priced while others are free. East End Life paper is also delivered free through doors.

The award ceremonies were introduced by community organisations and a few individuals who realised the need and importance of recognising the people, their members or institutions for their excellence, innovative ideas, creativity and acknowledging their significant contribution and achievements in society or relevant businesses.

On behalf of Canary Wharf Group, Zakir Khan first introduced the accolades of community champions on 26 October 2015. The first batch of recipients were Baroness Uddin, S B Faruk, Gulam Mostafa and Ex-Mayor Abdul Aziz Sardar.

Ex-councillor Abdal Ullah and Ayesha Qureshi first introduced the British-Bangladeshi Power and Inspiration 100 in January 2012; a celebration of the success of the Bangladeshi community in the UK today. Dilara Khan started to recognise mothers through an event known as Maa Amar Maa. London Tigers, a professional community organisation, recognises the achievements of young people in sports and encourages the children of different colour and faith groups to grow up together, keep away from bad influences, such as gangs, and fulfil their dreams. Mesbha Ahmed formed this unique organisation in 1986 and every year they organise award ceremonies and invite high profile people from across London.

The different associations came up with their way of distributing different awards to different people in different categories. Brick Lane restaurant associations also have a history of rewarding businesses in various categories in their famous curry festivals. The unique idea of Bangla Town Restaurants Association to organise curry festivals and serve street food, vitalises the local economy so much that they are held every year. They attract visitors and tourists from far and wide, supporting local restaurants and making Brick Lane a cornucopia of Bangladeshi cuisines.

John Biggs, Mayor of Tower Hamlets, recently announced that the Boishakhi Mela will be returning to Brick Lane and Weavers Field.

Although a few organisations are sometimes criticised for showing favouritism, most are very efficient, professional and genuine to my knowledge. Most associations like Bangladesh Caterers Association, Federation of Bangladesh Caterers, The Curry Life, Who's Who, Asian Business Awards, the Tiffin Club, Channel S and many other organisations, have their own regular annual awards and gala dinners. Many others including BBCC and Pillar Productions also organise award ceremonies and gala dinners, but not every year.

Bangladeshis not only participate in Bengali run competitions, but they also take part in mainstream TV competitions such as Lord Sugar's Apprentice. Sylheti young hijabi woman Nurun Ahmed participated in this popular show. Nadya, another Sylheti hijabi young woman fought off other competitors and won the Great British Bake Off in October 2015.

Every organisation and its organisers put in a great deal of effort, ideas, skill, experience and knowledge to make their events more memorable, more enjoyable and more remarkable. They certainly invest a huge amount of money and effort into organising these award evenings and prestigious gala dinners and invite dignitaries from different sectors each year.

British-Bangladesh Chamber of Women Entrepreneurs

I was honoured to be invited and to attend some prestigious events organised by many community organisations. It was a privilege to act as the only Bangladeshi judge in the British Curry Awards for the past three years, along with other dignified and independent judges from the mainstream community. I find the British Curry Awards to be an exclusive global platform, where the organisers demonstrate their ability to make the annual event much bigger, brighter and more forward thinking. I like their high profile programmes which are impressive and smart. Their judging process is robust, impartial and transparent. It is an event of excellence and inspiration and is a forum for thousands of guests to network, exchange views, share experiences and enjoy a glittering night at Battersea Evolution. Certainly, it is a great night for caterers, the community and the country. No wonder, the country's Prime Minister, The Rt Honourable David Cameron, said that the British Curry Awards is the Oscar of the curry industry.

The Founder of the British Curry Awards, Mr Enam Ali, MBE, FIH, is a visionary, diligent, principled person with infinite ideas who is determined to take the curry industry to a new height.

I think that at any award event, participants have the opportunity to showcase their innovative ideas and skills and demonstrate their creativity through competition. Even if they are not successful, they are inspired and encouraged to participate in the next event to try and win an award or accolade. Even the organisers have their own opportunities to improve and compete with each other, without challenging each other or creating bitterness, so that it becomes a win-win situation for all the caterers and their beloved industry. I strongly believe that if there is cooperation, collaboration and coordination among the organisers, and harmony and brotherhood among the caterers, many of its problems could be resolved slowly and gradually, but surely and certainly.

They have many common problems: chefs, reluctance of the younger generation to work unsocial hours, staff shortages, VAT, directives from Brussels on food safety, compulsory documentation, language barriers, training, lack of banking facilities and so on. These issues could be raised in a unified voice at award events when all the organisers invite, lobby and relay their messages to policy makers in the presence of VIPs, CIPs, MPs, mayors, ambassadors, High Commissioners, diplomats, celebrities, community leaders, caterers and even the Prime Minister. They can use their own ideas for organising events, but as far as everyday problems are concerned, a common approach is very much needed.

Mother Teresa said, 'I can do things you cannot. You can do things I cannot. Together we can do great things'.

Prime Minister David Cameron and Enam Ali, MBE announcing the winners at British Curry Awards

Three Judges of the British Curry Awards

Racism Now and Then

Brick Lane has seen a lot of hatred, bickering, fighting and racial tension, including the hurling of racist abuse on many occasions, which I witnessed in the mid-seventies. As mentioned previously, I was also the victim of racial attack in 1976.

On 4 May 1978, Altab Ali was murdered by three racist teenagers in broad daylight in Adler Street, a few minutes' walk from Brick Lane. He was walking home to Reardon Street from his place of work at a Brick Lane factory. Killing this innocent man was a turning point for Bangladeshis and others to unite and fight against racism. Thousands of people marched from Whitechapel to Whitehall behind Altab Ali's coffin and demonstrated against racist violence. The National Front (NF) moved their headquarters from West London to East London near Brick Lane after Altab Ali's murder. However, due to the combined campaign and protest by Brick Lane youths, they eventually moved out.

From 48 Brick Lane, I witnessed how strong and active our youths were in those days. I cannot remember many names, but certainly remember a few of them who are still around. Shirajul Haque Shiraj, Rajon Uddin Jalal, Syed

Mizan, Ataur Rahman Ata, Rarique Ullah, Ex-Cllr Alauddin, Ayub Karam Ali, the late Barik bhai, Ex Deputy Mayor Akikur Rahman, Taimus Ali, Konor bhai, Osman Gani, Abdus Salique, Shafik bhai, Aftab Ali, Kutub bhai, Nuruddin bhai, Nizam bhai, Mr Abdul Mukit Chunu, Syed Nurul, Ex Cllr Joynal, Ala Miah Azad, Ana Miah, Dr Zahid Hassan, Ex-Cllr Enamul Haque, Late Dr Haris Ali, Gulam Yahia, Rahim Boksh and others played vital roles, protected the interests and safety of their community and helped to remove the racist headquarters from Brick Lane. Their movement resulted in the introduction of a small police station in Brick Lane for first time.

In 1994, the Council named a park after Altab Ali as a memorial to where he was murdered. Even today, this park is used for an assembly point for many kinds of demonstrations, whether relating to Bangladeshi issues or any other issues affecting people here or in Bangladesh.

On 23 October 2015, John Biggs the Executive Mayor of LBTH, announced from Altab Ali Park that 4th May would be known as Altab Ali Day. This was appreciated by the people of Brick Lane, but Dabir Miah, a friend of late Altab Ali, expressed his sorrow that no one was caring about the family of Altab Ali who are still mourning his loss and living in distress in a village near Chattak, Sunamganj.

As mentioned in the introduction, skinheads, the National Fronts (NF) and the British National Party (BNP) used to come to Brick Lane in their respective groups, visibly brandishing weapons. They would physically assault and verbally abuse the innocent Bangladeshis and others. There was no police station in Brick Lane at that time. The nearest one was in Mansel Street, which closed down long ago. Even the Bethnal Green police station has closed down. Now we have at least a small police booth in the middle of Brick Lane, which has been serving the community and assuring the safety of the neighbourhood.

When the NF attacked without any notice, it was difficult to report to the police as not many residents had access to landline phones at that time, let alone mobile phones, which had not been invented. Helplessly, we had to rely on God or any other help to come to our rescue. 48 Brick Lane where I used to live upstairs was regularly attacked. They would throw stones, break the windows and hurl foul language. They would phone your business number at odd hours. If you did not answer, it would keep on ringing and disturb your sleep. Phone receivers had no mute option in them. If you picked the phone up, you would hear, 'Paki bashi' abuse. There were no people on the streets of Brick Lane to come to your aid. The only solution was to look after yourself, lock yourself up in your room and watch black and white TV for a while before going to bed. Jamme Mosque in particular was their key target, because it was the main hub of the community. Today, they target East London Mosque and Whitechapel because of mass congregation.

In 1982, I remember being allocated a council flat not far away from Brick Lane. It was near Cambridge Heath Road. The estate caretaker showed us around the flat at 30 Barbanel House, Cephas Street, London E1. It was really a beautiful, tastefully decorated corner flat on the top floor, so without hesitation we decided to take it and move in. Unfortunately, as we concluded our visit and exited the flat, a tall, well-built Englishman, came out from next door and very angrily pointed his finger to the caretaker and said, 'If you make these people my next door neighbours, I will kill them.' That's exactly what he said. Obviously, we were very scared. Our momentary dream was shattered. We were stunned to hear such a racist remark and verbal threat before we had even moved in. We were not expecting to experience such hatred, nor were we used to such scenarios. The caretaker was himself an Englishman. He was very helpful and friendly and while walking down the stairs he assured us not to worry about the neighbour. He said, 'Take your time and don't take him seriously.'

We were given few days to decide. We were in a dilemma. On one hand we liked the flat and desperately needed it, but on the other hand, the next door neighbour was so rude and threatening. We were trying to decide what to do and after a few days of deep thought, we finally decided to accept it as a challenge and take the flat. However, beforehand, we also decided to talk nicely to our arrogant next door neighbour and cool him down. If this therapy worked, we would take the flat, otherwise we would forget it. After couple of days, we knocked on the door at 29. The same guy opened the door and came out. Behind him was his wife. We said hello to both. I said that we had visited the flat the other day and saw that he was a bit upset. We explained and assured them that we would be good neighbours and not to worry about us. They complained that the previous Bangladeshi family used to cook very strong and smelly curry and were very noisy too. I understood what they meant and assured them this wouldn't happen in our case. Our friendly discussion was very helpful. They cooled down. We were so relieved and believed that although argument decides who is right, discussion decides what is right. We were right to talk to them. We found them totally different than the previous time. They would definitely be our good neighbours.

We moved in with all our belongings and stayed in Barbanel House for nearly three years before buying our own freehold property. Within that time, we demonstrated what considerate neighbours we could be. We proved ourselves to be the best possible next door neighbours. Our neighbours at 29 became our good friends. We used to leave our door key with them before going to Bangladesh on holiday. Who would believe that the people we thought were racists would become such great neighbours, with whom we coexisted so happily for years. During our absence, they used to water our plants, collect our post and looked after the flat as if it were their own. We used to invite them in for tea and treated them with our curry, which once they disliked. Soon they liked the curry and even asked for it sometimes. We used to give them Christmas cards, New Year gifts and things like that. We learnt that integration really works. If you do not intermingle and attempt to communicate with others from different communities and racial groups, the misunderstanding will remain. It will creep up in some other form.

Today, after all these years, I find that racism has taken a different twist. Racism and religion are in conflict. What was previously visible racism has now become invisible too in the shape of Islamophobia, which is now on the cutting edge of racism.

The nail bomb in Brick Lane in 1997, the 7/7 bombing in Aldgate in 2005, the 9/11 tragedy in New York, anti-immigrant hostility, the ripple effects of the 'shock and awe' Iraq war, the Trojan horse case in Birmingham schools in 2014, the brutal killing of innocent Palestinians by Israeli soldiers and Muslims joining the war in Syria are just a few examples. Then there are the problems in the Middle East, the beheading of American journalist James Foley in August 2014 by an alleged Muslim who reportedly lives in East London, the execution of a British soldier in broad daylight in a London street in Woolwich, the ban on hijabs in France, attacks on Muslim women wearing hijabs in Whitechapel, and attacks on mosques including East London Mosque etc., some of which are covert signs of the intense racism and hatred now affecting society. It was never like this before. These are affecting all communities in general, but the Muslim community in particular, not only in Brick Lane, but elsewhere too.

The racist attacks in the past were not as widespread as they are now. It was quite common to witness racial attacks by the extremists from other side of Brick Lane near Bethnal Green Road. Now Brick Lane is relatively safe. Our younger generation are integrating more with mainstream community. There is mutual understanding and more unification than before. Brick Lane is alive around the clock; restaurants are busy serving their customers, worshippers are busy going to the Jamme Mosque to queue up for prayers behind the Imam. In the daytime, shops are busy, mothers are taking their kids to Christchurch School and tourists are grouping together to listen to their guide talking about historic sites in Brick Lane. Things have changed for better. We have a police station and more 'bobbies on the beat'. Mobile phones are available to everyone, there are more streetlights, more CCTV cameras, more security, greater safety and strict laws.

However, invisible hatred, institutional racism and Islamophobia are now felt everywhere, which is extremely worrying and much more alarming than that which I experienced myself in the 1970s. I once found the Marble Arch tube station closed because of the IRA bombing in 1976 and I heard the roaring sound of a bomb blast in Canary Wharf in 1996. This kind of terrorist activity seems to have died down. Today, you don't see actions from the NF (National Front) that often, but still face threats from the EDL (English Defence League) and other extremist groups. They come in their hundreds to attack mosques, not only in East London but in other Muslim areas too. Today, you can see the British press hysterically encourages Islamophobia, exacerbates community tension and divides the media and Muslims.

In August 2014, the front page of the Daily Express read: 'Muslims tell us how to run our Schools'. The Daily Star wrote: 'BBC Put Muslims Before You'. The Times printed: 'Rise in Muslim birthrate as families "feel British"'. I think these are counter-productive, dangerous, discriminatory and hostile towards Muslim community. This worries me and I am concerned for our next generation. I survived the physical racist attack on myself, but it has left me scarred. What will happen to my kids? They may not experience physical attacks as I did, but they might have to live with the permanent scar of discreet racism, which will hurt them even more.

The Gaza protest in August 2014 in Brick Lane, Leeds, Manchester, Scotland and many other parts of Britain, may have upset groups other than Muslims and generated discreet hatred in various communities. It may even have damaged the very fabric of multicultural society. At this volatile time of the year, even HSBC bank closed down the accounts of a few Muslim organisations. It certainly caused concern for both the young and elderly generations.

I can boycott the products of some countries I don't like, but I cannot change the regime. That's what is worrying me and many other fellow Muslims I know, from Brick Lane to Brook Lynn. Now, when in underground stations, I hide the free newspaper headlines, which write boldly about Muslim extremism. I feel ashamed to expose that page to fellow passengers, although every passenger already has the same free paper. They don't talk with each other, unlike Bangladeshis who love to share their views and even debate issues whilst travelling on the bus, train or boat, or sitting in restaurants and cafés. English people are different. They read a book or newspaper quietly. They won't talk to fellow passengers and they get off the train or bus quietly. Even our children who were born and brought up here in UK do the same. Unlike my generation, they will not stop to watch a fight on the street for example; they will just walk away.

Back home in Bangladesh, we will try to find the cause of any problem and engage in reasoning, but our children are different. I noticed this habit with my own son Safwan. I once asked him to buy something from our corner shop. He went to a different corner shop in the opposite direction. It was a bit bizarre to me. When I asked him why he chose the other shop, he did not reply. His mum later told me that many months earlier he had encountered a few unruly boys on this side and since then he had avoided that corner. I shared this story with a college friend of mine, Mohiuddin Choudhury, whose son is the same age as Safwan. My friend said his son was once involved with an altercation with friends while playing rugby. During the game, he was racially abused and since then he stopped playing rugby, although he was a very good player in that team. Since those incidents, he never went to the field, nor took part in the sports he once loved. This illustrates that our children do not want to protest, nor become involved in any dispute. They prefer to be left alone and suffer silently. I think our younger generation should not ignore it. They must stand up and raise their voices; they must protest to protect themselves. They need to mix more with others, try to understand each other and not suffer in silence. I know that racism is still alive and kicking. My generation saw it in one way and our current generation is experiencing it in a different way.

Let me now narrate a story that I will never forget. Everyone knows what happened on Tuesday 11 September 2001, now known as 9/11. The World Trade Centre (Twin Towers) where my family and I visited once was destroyed by two hijacked passenger planes, killing thousands of innocent people for reasons and motives not known to me until now. What is clear to me now is that it had a lasting impact on people from Brooklyn to Brick Lane and countries from East to West. What happened to its mastermind, Osama Bin Laden, is now history. This sort of skyjacking and the use of passengers as hostages is unparalleled and will certainly remain embedded in history for ever.

Similarly, after 9/11, an incident happened in a school near Brick Lane, which will remain embedded in my memory too. I was a prospective parliamentary candidate at that time from Bethnal Green and Bow constituency, which includes Brick Lane and represents the constituents in the vicinity of Brick Lane. One day, while in my office at Princelet Street, off Brick Lane, I received a phone call from my friend Sattar bhai from Rajmahal Sweet Shop, Brick Lane. He sounded desperate and sought my help. I did not have a clue as to what help he was seeking, but suggested that he come down to my office, which was a stone's throw from his shop. He came down immediately.

I asked him what I could do for him. He said that one of his relatives had a problem in his school. His relative was only 15 and was a student of St. Paul's Secondary School. He was having serious trouble with the headmaster and others in the school. I listened carefully and suggested that he go as a guardian and sort it out. He said he had a language problem and wanted me to go. I told him that I could go and help with translation only. He then said that the boy's father was cutting his visit short and returning from Bangladesh the following day after hearing about the incident. I asked why it was so serious that his father had to come back from his holiday. He asked me to accompany the student and his father and they would explain everything. I would just need to translate for them.

I found it a bit weird, but since I was supposed to help out my constituents, I agreed. The father and son came to my office by mini cab the following day and asked me to accompany them. I had never met them before, nor did I have any clue what was going on. In the car, I wanted to find out what had happened to him in school. The boy remained silent and did not say a single word. I asked his father, an OAP, who had no knowledge of what had occurred. He lived a pensioner's life in Bangladesh and only travelled over after receiving a phone call saying that something serious had happened in school involving his son, who was from his second marriage.

I didn't bother them much, as I was supposed to interpret only. When we arrived in front of school gate and got out of the cab, we met with the headmaster and a few others who were expecting us. They asked whether the student's father was Mr Ali and he confirmed that he was. The headmaster shook hands with me and I introduced myself. He took us to a room and gave us chairs to sit on. Other people, including two uniformed police officers, joined in. I now realised it had something to do with a serious crime. The headmaster started the meeting and asked me first whether I knew why I was there. I told him I didn't.

He then said, 'This boy was in the examination hall and was supposed to answer the exam questions. But instead of answering any question, he drew something on the exam sheet.'

He opened the exam sheet and showed us. On the front page he had drawn a tall tower. On one side he had drawn an aircraft hitting the tower and on another side he had written the name of Osama bin Laden. The school authorities took it very seriously and viewed it as an act of terrorism. They involved the police. They sent a letter to the boy's guardian who had to come back all the way from Bangladesh to attend this trial. I found myself in a very awkward situation. I never expected nor even imagined this sort of incident. The atmosphere in the room became very tense. Normally, I would have imagined this to be the silly act of a silly school kid. He could have been cautioned, but they treated him like a young terrorist and involved the school head, the form tutor, the law enforcing authority and others. They thought this boy was a potential terrorist and left no stone unturned in trying to find out why he did it.

The boy didn't answer and remained silent. His father started to cry and spoke in Bengali, which I translated into English. He said he had a lot of respect for Britain, had served in the Second World War for Britain and now his own son was being treated like this, which was unfair.

The headmaster concluded the meeting by saying that the guardian would be informed of the outcome of the meeting by post. Later, I heard that he was barred from sitting with other students, sat exams on his own and would receive an adverse school report. That meant his future was bleak. This certificate would have an adverse impact on his future employment too. Someone said he was harshly punished because the school head was an American and the form tutor was a Jew. I personally do not think it had anything to do with anyone's nationality or religion. However, from that day I realised that the ripple effect of 9/11 has reached Brick Lane.

Almost ten years after the incident, I met Sattar bhai in Brick Lane Mosque and out of curiosity asked him about the boy who was punished for his offence in the examination room. He said the boy had been suffering from mental illness, had spent lot of time in hospital, but recovered a little and was released from hospital. I heard that his father had since passed away.

Today, in 2015, a similar story of a 14-year-old Muslim school student hit the head line of the world press when he was arrested and handcuffed in Texas, US for bringing a homemade clock to school for his homework. The teacher thought it was a hoax bomb and the police were called. Although he was later released, the story went viral through social media. Mohammad's father later withdraw him from this school. President Barak Obama even invited the boy to the White House, but the damage had already been done.

We have to remember that no one is born racist. It is a social menace. To minimise or eradicate this social menace, every single citizen - be it a student, teacher or anyone in any profession - must play their collective role. They must all take responsibility and demonstrate their tolerance. They have to integrate with each other. We must all unite against it, otherwise this disease will spread rapidly and become uncontrollable. In the past, we tackled it individually. Then the youth front stood against it collectively in Brick Lane and it worked. Even today, when the EDL comes in a flock, every community (black, white, Asians, MCB) and many other organisations tackle the racists in one united front. That's how we can collectively protect the community. We should also educate our younger generation to integrate more with people of other faith groups and other communities. From the school playground to the workplace, children and adults should meet and greet each other and form friendly bonds.

Teacher-student relationships must be improved. The Government has to do more to include religious tolerance and social integration on the educational curriculum. For every action, there is an opposite reaction. This is true in science and politics too. If the UK Government shows too much support for Israel, Muslim frustration will be felt at home. They should maintain a balanced approach on Middle East policy. I think that might help to stop the 'home grown terrorists' as the Government terms them.

I tried and succeeded in softening the attitude of my next door neighbour and formed a great friendship with him over 30 years ago, so others can do the same. Even the Government can bring about change in society, however small that change might be. We also have to try ourselves. Public Private Effort could minimise the tension of racism in society, otherwise it will engulf society and pose a real risk to everyone. Hence proactive policies such as raising awareness and educating society are paramount. Nelson Mandela rightly said, 'Education is the most powerful weapon which you could use to change the world'.

Let's share our bad experiences, learn from past mistakes and educate ourselves to build a better community free from racism, prejudice or hatred of any kind or shape. Only then can we hope for a better future for our children who will benefit from our investment in our communities.

Family, Festivals and Fun

The Bangladeshi population did not bring their families when waves of immigrants started to settle near Brick Lane in the 60s. They lived mainly in the area of Hunton Place, near Brick Lane, which includes council estates like Arthur Deakin House, Mcglashon House, Stuttle House and others. Hunton Place is now called Hunton Street, whose residency is one hundred percent Bangladeshis. They started to apply for their families to join them and I saw the Sylheti families coming up in the early 70s. They have now settled and colonised the whole area and made it their permanent and predominant place. They established a connectivity between house and home. They never forgot their roots and set an example of their bonding between their home country and host country.

I owned an electronic and video shop adjacent to Hunton Street. I had many customers, mainly the new arrival mothers from Bangladesh. Some of them probably did not even see the City of Dhaka before they saw the City of London. I was surprised to see these young women who could not speak correct Bengali language, but would soon speak in fluent Hindi, Urdu and English. Most of them picked up Hindi and Urdu from films and dramas. They realised the need and importance of learning the language of the land and soon learnt it. Their motivation and determination to learn foreign languages worked, because they knew that unless they learnt English, they would be handicapped. While their husbands were out and about, they would do their shopping and other daily chores. They were motivated to learn English and other languages and soon developed their skill, experience, confidence and knowledge.

Many women took up jobs of tailoring in their own homes. They worked very hard day in, day out. The rag trade was flourishing in Brick Lane at that time. Men and women alike were working around the clock to earn money. Unfortunately, the rag trade has now nearly died out. Only a handful of factories are now in operation and most have moved out of Brick Lane. Panache Outwear Ltd is the only surviving company doing well in its modern factory from Bromley by Bow. The Managing Director is Sayed Ahmed and the company is still manufacturing ladies' and gents' coats for branded names such as Burberry.

The rag trade has now been replaced by the restaurant trade. Now second or third generations are working hard in this business. Unlike their elders, they don't employ their families. The seniors are now either on a pension or have moved out of the area to live elsewhere in their second home. Many of them took up the offer of the 'right to buy' scheme. They bought council properties at a reduced price and moved out, but still maintained the ownership of businesses and a few retained contact with Brick Lane. Many families invested their hard earned money on their children's education. The younger generation are now doing well outside of Brick Lane, either in the City or the West End. Some of the older generation, who were unable to communicate in English and sought the help of interpreters, now find their children working for organisations like HSBC, NatWest, Barclays, the Post Office, Tesco, Sainsbury, Asda, Argos and so on. These workplaces are a short distance from Brick lane. Many of the younger generation have become barristers, solicitors, lawyers and journalists and either work for big companies or have established their own businesses in and around Brick Lane.

Families are growing and their expenditure is increasing too. The older generation had a tendency to remit their hard earned money from Brick Lane to Bangladesh. They built large houses and bought land, but now most of them are regretting their unproductive investments.

The younger generation, on the other hand, are also working hard but investing their money in buying properties here in Britain rather than in Bangladesh. They are taking a more positive move and prudently investing their money in the right staff at the right time.

Marriages used to take place between relatives or families known to each other. The older generation preferred to take their sons and daughters back to Bangladesh and arrange marriages within their extended families. Some of these marriages worked out, but unfortunately many others did not. Today's new generation would like to get married here in the UK, preferably to someone of their own choice. Now marriages are not only taking place among only Sylheti communities, but also between Sylheti, non-Sylheti, Pakistani and even other communities and other nationalities.

Marriage is now an expensive event. Our community has a tendency to spend huge sums of money when it is not necessary. They will spend thousands of pounds on one single day on a wedding. The knot-tying event is an enormous extravagance. It costs families an extraordinary amount for prestigious venues, ornaments and jewellery, car and limousine hire, expensive meals, clothes, costumes, HR filming, photography furniture, sound systems, music, multi-tiered cakes and fruit tree decorations etc. In the old days, people used to hire a restaurant or community centre for a few hours. It included food, drinks and service etc., which served its purpose. Even today, Sonargao Restaurant in Brick Lane caters for weddings, yet many families are opting for five star hotels, banqueting halls, marquees and horse drawn carriages. Some are even hiring helicopters. This is sometimes unnecessary and a sheer waste of money, which puts tremendous hardship on many families. Their life savings become a life burden, with worries about debt repayment. They should check their balance sheet before embarking on such a spending spree. This needs to be addressed by families, who need to find a way to provide a more modest option instead of lavish and over-priced weddings.

Brick Lane is a hub for Indian food. The Bangladeshi restaurants are now dotted the length and breadth of Brick Lane, but in the early 70s I saw only handful of restaurants there. The most well-known and busy restaurants were Clifton and Salimar, owned by Musa Patel who has now passed away. Then it was Nirala and Sweet and Spice. All of them have either closed down, changed ownership or been renamed. Sweet and Spice was once one of the most popular restaurants for local factory workers and visitors. It was quite affordable and it was my favourite place for Halwa and Puri. Unfortunately, this has now changed hands and is offering different menus with different names.

Clifton Restaurant on the middle of Brick Lane was mainly used by English customers. It was popular for its famous Indian and Pakistani dishes and lunchtimes and evenings were equally busy. This restaurant is now owned by Azmol Hussain and trading under the name of Preeti Restaurant. He owns another restaurant called Preem.

Salamar was another good restaurant. It was also owned by the late Musa. It was famous for Roti and meat Bhuna. Café Naz, Akash, Salimar, Clifton and Tajmahal have now closed down. Other existing restaurants are Aladin, Radhuni, Amar Gao, Gram Bangla, Nazrul, Café Grill, Sheba, Cinnamon, Shampan, Famous Curry Bazaar, Khusboo, The Famous Moonlight, Café Bangla, Muhib, Eastern Eye, Meraz, Mango, Sonargaon, Saffron, Monsoon, Papadoms, Standard Balti House, Bengal Village, Chillies, Masala, Curry Capital, Al Badar, Brick Lane Brasserie, Clipper, Shaad Grill and Bangladeshi Restaurant, Bengal Cuisine, Bangla Oven, Gandhi's and Rajmahal.

There is a large cluster of Bangladeshi restaurants in and around Brick Lane.

These restaurants are not only catering for the needs of the local customers, but are also attracting customers from far and wide who are given the best food for the best price and the traditional hospitality of Bangladesh. I think that Brick Lane curry houses need to add different world dishes to their menus to meet the changing tastes of customers, which would help attract more business. Brick Lane needs to be seen as a place that can bring all the communities together. It needs to incorporate Osborne Street into it; a small street should not be left on its own. Merging with Brick Lane would make it easier for customers and tourists to enter the lane from Aldgate East and Whitechapel undergrounds.

Brick Lane Restaurant Association is a voice for all restaurateurs. It looks after the interests of all restaurant owners in Brick Lane. Sadly, they cannot unite to stop the touting, which is damaging the reputation of the restaurants and Brick Lane too. Some restaurants were even fined by the local council for illegal touting. This sort of touting was never seen in Brick Lane in the past. It's a recent phenomenon to pull the passing customers in by giving false offers. This sometimes creates rivalry among the fellow restaurateurs, which leads to bitterness and sometimes involvement with the police. This culture of persistent and aggressive touting must be stopped for the sake of business, reputation, environment and law. Otherwise the area will attract more negative publicity, deter customers, kill businesses and damage the local economy for good. In order to restore the old image of the area, the restaurants should seriously take a collective approach to terminate this unpleasant touting culture. Even the local Bangladeshi residents feel ashamed to see this ugly touting taking place in front of their own eyes.

Residents of Brick Lane also make complaints to the local authority about the noise created by some drunken customers late at night. Some of these customers even urinate in front of residents' doors. Although Brick Lane is a tourist hotspot, there are no public toilets. The local residents complain a great deal to the council, so the council has now decided not to allow the restaurants to stay open too late at night. Ironically, a few decades ago, those who used to blame elderly Bangladeshis for chewing betel leaf and spitting on the street in the day time, are the ones now blamed for blighting the same street at night time. My neighbour, Askor Miah of 45 Princelet Street, was disgusted by the attitude of the people urinating on the street, doors and shop shutters and complained to me on numerous occasions. It was also reported in local papers and TV channels.

Amidst negative news, there is considerable positive news for the community of Brick Lane and outsiders too. Brick Lane has proudly presented and introduced Mela for the first time. It has attracted people from all walks of life. Now it is duplicated from Brick Lane to Barking, Birmingham and other cities, including a few European cities. Credit goes to many within the Boishakhi Mela Trust, but mainly to Shirajul Haque Shiraj who contributed hugely to the introduction of this Mela from Brick Lane. Bangladeshis simply love to enjoy it. They come in flocks to celebrate the Bengali New Year. It has proven to be the largest, innovative open-air festival outside of Bangladesh.

Brick Lane definitely achieves its recognition and reputation from such performance, presentation, production and participation of local, national and international skill, knowledge, culture, music, amusements, enjoyment, dance, networking and other attractions. To me, this is an event of the community, by the community, for the community. The Mela has shifted from Brick

Lane to Allen Gardens to Altab Ali Park and now Victoria Park.

Brick Lane Illumination Association took the initiative to illuminate and brighten up Brick Lane with lighting for different festivals, mainly during Eid, Diwali and Christmas. Now we can enjoy similar lighting during different festivals in different parts of Newham's Green Street and Stratford etc.

Brick Lane also attracted a lot of foreigners during the restaurant food festival. Local restaurants took part in the competition where local chefs demonstrated their skills and displayed their curries to a panel of judges, who awarded the winners with prizes. Although this is not like the British Curry Awards, Curry Life Awards, Federation of Bangladeshi Caterers or Bangladesh Caterers Association Awards, its uniqueness is closing Brick Lane to traffic and opening it up for pedestrians. It allows the local restaurateurs to take part in open cooking and displays and to enjoy their food outside all along Brick Lane. Brick Lane gets the opportunity to showcase their local skills, promote their local experts, boost the local economy and act as catering ambassadors to both national and foreign visitors and tourists.

Taj Stores

The Taj Stores in Brick Lane is a household name for Bangladeshis. It is not only the oldest business set up by a Bangladeshi in Brick Lane, but is a landmark and visitors' attraction too. In the early 80s, Taj Stores was the business next door to my 'Shahnan Showbiz'. Even today, my business 'Shahnan Training' and Taj Stores are separated by a small common backyard only. They serve all the communities with a wide range of groceries and a broad spectrum of fresh fruit and vegetables imported from Bangladesh and other countries. As a neighbour and customer, I have known this remarkable store serving its customers with pride, honesty, integrity and discharging its corporate social responsibility too. The essence of this store is that they have earned and retained their respect and reputation for many decades.

This store used to be widely known as 'Jabbar's Shop' after the name of its founder, the late Abdul Jabbar who opened the shop in 1936. I never met him, as he died many years before my arrival in Brick Lane. He is in the history books now and I have read many articles and stories on him in numerous magazines and newspapers. However, I was lucky to know his brothers; the late Alhaj Abdul Khalique and Abdul Rahman. Both brothers were very polite, gentle, religious and well mannered. They were well-to-do, but very down to earth people. Mr Abdur Rahman looked after his Beauty Saree shop in Brick Lane next to my shop some thirty years ago. In those days, there were a few saree shops in Brick Lane; today, there are none.

Alhaj Abdul Khalique was a regular worshipper in Brick Lane Jamme Mosque. He was never late for his prayer and I had the opportunity to perform prayer together with him. Sadly, he passed away in 1994. This international store is now carried forward by the present generation of three brothers; Juned, Jamal and Joynal. They are successfully flying the flag of their family. Taj Stores is now one of the biggest superstores in Brick Lane and a major employer in the area. They create jobs and employ a large number of people from the local community. At the same time, the three polite, humble and gentle 'J's' are following in the footsteps of their previous generation, upholding the name and fame their elders left behind, enriching Brick Lane and its community and continuously expanding their business and contributing to local and national economy.

Learning and Earning

I know a lot of people who came to the UK from Bangladesh as economic migrants, but a vast proportion had the intention of returning to their country. A few did, but most of them changed their mind and fully settled down here. Initially they wanted to come here to work, earn some money, build houses back home and support their families financially, but later realised that their investments in land, bricks and mortar were not only futile, but were causing serious family disputes and often breaking up families. Now, they tend to sell their properties back home, bring their monies here and live a better life with their families in the UK. In doing so, many of them are facing legal difficulties and wasting foreign currency on bribing police, courts, pleaders and even political leaders to some extent. It is too late for most of them. However, there are other people who are investing in different sectors, making more money more than they used to make here in UK and are living there happily like kings.

In 1974, I remember being asked by a friend of mine whether I would return to Bangladesh or stay here permanently. I said that after only one year I would go back to my beloved Bangladesh. Now, more than forty years later, I am still here in my beloved Brick Lane and would never ever dream of going back to the country where I was born and still have family, friends and properties.

I think 'earning and learning' have no ending. As a small child, I was asked by my father what the ultimate limit of my academic qualification would be when I grew up. I do not know the answer I gave to my father, but he later reminded me that my answer was, 'I will read the last lesson of this world'. I was wrong as a child. Now I know that there is nothing called the 'last lesson' as such. Learning has no limits. As an OAP, I am still learning; it's a continuous process.

I also learnt something new on the first day of my arrival in England in 1973. It was my duty to inform my parents of my arrival in a new country, among new people and in a new environment. So, I went to the post office to send a telegram to my father in Sunamganj. In those days, the quickest way of communication was via telegram. Posting letters would take about two weeks, so I decided to send a telegram with the shortest possible message to cut the cost down. The longer your message, the more you had to pay. It was not like today's email or text messages that you can send and receive immediately, or even Skype and

97

Facetime where you can see someone while you are chatting to them. It was very time consuming and costly in those days. It required form filling, standing in a queue, handing it over the counter and paying the fee etc.

I completed a form and wrote my message with only two words: 'REACHED SAFELY'. I handed the form to the young girl behind the post office counter. She took a look, corrected my writing, wrote something on a new form and handed it back to me for my signature. On it, she had written: 'ARRIVED SAFELY'. I smiled, put my signature on the form and gave it back to the girl. She signed and sealed it, took the fees and gave me a receipt.

I came home and told myself that this was the first lesson I had learnt in the UK from a young girl. Now I know that this small global village is nothing but a big kindergarten. Here we learn every single day. There is no last lesson. There is no age limit to learning.

On another occasion, about thirty-two years ago, I went to Sobur bhai's flat in Danvers House, Christian Street, London E1 with my friend Taufiqul Ambia Choudhury. When Sobur bhai called us for dinner, his little son helped his mother arrange the table and told us, 'Please fill your station up'. I was so amazed to be addressed in a very new and different way from a 10-year-old boy. In Bangladesh, I would have said either, 'Please sit down' or 'Please take your seat'. But instead, the boy said, 'Please fill your station up'.

Sobur bhai has passed away, but he invested heavily in his children's education. No wonder his son, Omar Faruk, the small boy of yesterday, is now a practising barrister of today. There are many examples in our community today. Our older generation who had difficulties in communicating in English, who needed translators or interpreters, soon learnt English and managed themselves in shops, banks, post offices, markets and so on. Our Bangladeshi women also picked up the language quickly. They can speak good English, Hindi, Urdu, Arabic and French in Brick Lane, Britain in general, in Europe and the Middle East. They realised that 'necessity knows no bounds'. They had to learn in order to stay in the respective countries for good.

Nowadays, not many people need interpreters in the UK. Every house has at least one or more graduates. We have created a generation of educated youngsters and most are now engaged in professional jobs and are barristers, solicitors, doctors and engineers etc.

The community still believes in learning from this world classroom. On this long journey of learning, they constantly acquire knowledge, skills, ability, intelligence and talents. They have a strong religious faith and believe what the Holy Quran says: 'Travel as far as China to acquire knowledge'. I agree with my community and add a quote of Barbara Viniar: 'It is learning, individually and collectively, which makes us strong, gives us hope and carries us forward'.

The Bangladeshi community is carrying itself forward with name and fame, with the maturity and experience they have acquired over the decades, starting from seamen (Lascars) from Sylhet, India, Burma and China, who first settled here, and the fourth generation of Bangladeshis who were born, brought up and educated here.

Dadabhai Nouroji made his debut in 1892 by becoming the first Asian MP in Britain. He represented the Liberal Party from Central Finsbury. In 1895, Mr Mancherjee Bhownagree of Indian Parsee heritage, became a British Conservative MP for Bethnal Green. In 2010, Rushanara Ali, was the first Bangladeshi to be elected to the House of Commons by becoming the Labour MP for Bethnal Green and Bow.

History has already been made in politics by Bangladeshis. It is continuously moving forward and history will again define us for our hard work, dedication, determination, devotion, education and inspiration. The community can take pride in our younger generation for their motivation to compete with other communities in this challenging world. It could be from Brick Lane or beyond.

SsBA

The economic barometer of the Bangladeshi community in Banglatown certainly has a direct link with SsBA (Spitalfields Small Business Association) and impact from their continuous support and assistance. Bangladeshi SMEs and other community businesses in and around Brick Lane have achieved long term positive results and sustainability from the help and support from SsBA, which was established in 1979. The lifeline of Brick Lane's SMEs has largely been the SsBA, to which they owe their success. SsBA is a voluntary sector organisation that has helped local communities over the last few decades.

SsBA is not a charity or a profit-making organisation. Nevertheless, tenants are offered affordable rents and take control of their own businesses. As a member of SsBA since 1986, my business has benefited in a number of ways. My business at 103 Brick Lane was right opposite the old premises of SsBA at 107 Brick Lane. When the council demolished our businesses under the Planning and Compulsory Purchase Act, it was SsBA who came out to help and allocated me one of their units at 33 Princelet Street. Since then, they have provided me with a free computer, free unlimited internet, and a free website and are acting as my support system.

I am aware of many such small businesses in Spitalfields, which are receiving constant help and support from SsBA. Through SsBA's online service, the tenant members are embracing the potential of e-commerce and the World Wide Web. Tenant members of SsBA have access to a tailor-made internet and web portal 24/7. They also receive one-to-one support and guidance on the use of modern technology whenever needed. They provide free business advice and help to improve the lives of the local community too.

It is indeed an inspiring example of changing the economic progress and prosperity of an area, whilst working and motivating the communities to bring about positive changes in the local environment. It is a social enterprise with enduring commitment to deliver real and visible benefits to close-knit communities with their extensive experience of urban regeneration. They have not confined their knowledge, skills, consultancy and expertise within Banglatown, but have taken it as far as Japan. They also specialise in the renewal of rundown and unused space for retail, commercial or workshops.

They have developed a business support system and networking ability to help, support and strengthen the local community. The pioneers of SsBA Kay Jordan and Tassaduq Ahmed have both sadly passed away. Kay Jordan was a workaholic and Tassaduq Ahmed was a renowned figure within the Bangladeshi community. Both of them were near and dear to me and the present Chairman of SsBA, Mr Aziz Choudhury, attended the same college with me in Sylhet.

SsBA is helping all communities. One tenant, Gaziul Hasan Khan, had a small printing unit in Brick Lane. He later made his name and fame as a Minister for the Embassy of the People's Republic of Bangladesh in Washington DC. Other reputable and long standing members of SsBA include the British-Bangladesh Chamber of Commerce, Shahnan Employment and Training Bureau, Aerolex UK Ltd, Taj Accountants, Al-Amin Store, London Training Centre, Al-Amin Travels, Oriental Contracting Co Ltd, Dorpon Media Service, Sunrise Wedding Services Ltd, Hussain Tailoring, Frame Land, Miame, Janomot Newsweekly, Parents' Centre, Osmani Cultural Trust, Shah Monwar Ali Sunni Madrasa, Fairkey, Sabbir Travel & Job Centre and Heba Women's Project etc.

Mr Fairkey, Gulam Kibria, Eddie and Chanu Miah are actively involved with SsBA. SsBA has lost Tasadduk Ahmed, Kay Jordan, Peter and Askondar Ali, all of whom will be sadly missed.

SsBA organised a condolence meeting at BDC to remember Kay Jordan

Old Montague Street

One of the main arteries of Brick Lane is Old Montague Street. Unlike Hanbury Street, Princelet Street and Fashion Street, this has its own history and stories of transformation lasting nearly 150 years. A little over a century ago, this street used to be inhabited by the Jewish community. There were a number of synagogues and the population of Jews was 95 to 100 percent. Today, nearly the same percentage of the population is from the Muslim Bangladeshi community.

In the past, it was a small, narrow, dark road where a thin line of traffic used to flow. There were no yellow lines or parking meters and the width of the road was almost half that of today. It stretches from immediately opposite Sonali Bank, cutting Greatorex Street in half and eventually merging with Vallance Road.

Old Montague Street was purposely reconstructed in 1977, the purpose of which became clear to me one sunny day that year when I parked my car nearby and was walking down this street to reach my workplace at 48 Brick Lane. To my surprise, I saw something happening in front of the new, red-bricked Salvation Army building at 60 Old Montague Street. I stopped to see what was going on and saw a cohort of well-dressed aristocrats clearly waiting to welcome someone important. A few other onlookers joined me out of curiosity and we stood right opposite the group waiting on the pavement.

A black Rolls Royce took a right turn from Brick Lane and entered Old Montague Street, slowly pulling over on the right hand side. Someone opened the door and out stepped a lady, with a hat on her head, gloves on her hands and a handbag on her arm. It was Her Majesty the Queen who was greeted by all these aristocrats. Her Majesty cut the ribbon, officially opened the Salvation Army building and went inside.

There were not many police present, nor much security as there were no threats from Al Qaida or IS at that time. Everything was so effortless and everyone had their chance at least to glimpse Her Majesty from a short distance. It was indeed a historic moment for me, which I have not forgotten. One thing I noticed that there was no one from the Bangladeshi community in that host group to receive the Queen. That has now changed. If, for any reason, Her Majesty the Queen happens to visit the current Old Montague Street, or any other street within the Borough of Tower Hamlets, she will be received by someone who looks like me, talks like me and comes from same place as I come from in Bangladesh. That gentleman is none other than Abdul Mukit Chunu MBE, the First Citizen of the Borough, a Queen's representative and the Speaker of LBTH. Today, I would see most, if not all from Bangladeshi community, welcoming Her Majesty the Queen.

In later years, my wife and I were fortunate enough to be invited twice by the Chamberlain on behalf of Her Majesty the Queen to attend the Queen's Garden Party at Buckingham Palace twice. Unlike in 1977, when I saw her briefly from other side of a road, I saw her face-to-face at Her own Palace with HRH Prince Philip, Prince Charles and a few other members of the Royal Family. There were many Bangladeshis and their spouses who attended the Buckingham Palace Garden Parties and a few others who went there to receive awards such as the MBE and OBE etc.

This is just one of my personal experiences of Brick Lane, which is a clear demonstration of a changing community going from strength to strength. Her Majesty the Queen was greeted and received by the former Mayor of Tower Hamlets, Councillor Shafiqul Haque as part of protocol.

Today, we see Bangladeshis bringing name and fame to other places too. In 2015, at the time of writing, we have a Deputy Lord Mayor outside London; my friend Councillor Ali Ahmed who is now a Deputy Lord Mayor of Cardiff. From 2013-2014, Councillor Faruk Choudhury was Lord Mayor Elect of Bristol City.

Old Montague Street has certainly seen many changes, which I have witnessed. Whether more changes will occur remains to be seen. Its own name was changed in 1874 from Montague and Princes Street to today's Old Montague Street. It reminds me that change is inevitable, but British traditions remain the same. In the early 60s, when the Queen was invited to Dacca by the former President Field Marshal Muhammad Ayub Khan, the airport road was rebuilt to make it bigger and broader in honour of Her Majesty the Queen and was renamed New Airport Road. Similarly, I witnessed with my own eyes how Old Montague Street was rebuilt in the same way to honour Her Majesty in the mid-70s here in London.

Home to House (Bari to Basa)

In this chapter I am not defining the difference between 'home' and 'house', but a difference I have noticed between generations; my generation who were born in our 'home' in Bangladesh and my next generation who were born in our 'house' in England. I have noticed a significant difference in their thoughts and our thoughts. Our generation has immense love and attraction, feelings and emotions for their ancestral home (wherever it is) in Bangladesh.

Home to me is for living, not leaving. If you happen to leave home to live abroad, your love for home will be tripled. We would visit our home every year if we could afford it, but it is also difficult to convince our children to do this every year, even for a short visit to Bangladesh. I understand the reasons, such as safety, security, wellbeing and lack of amenities in a remote village to be visited by youngsters who are used to living in a much safer and more comfortable environment in the UK. However, even if we had modern houses built in bigger cities away from villages in Bangladesh, our children wouldn't feel comfortable or convinced. If there was equality in society, strict adherence of law and order, guaranteed assurance from the Government to attract our

110

younger generation to their mother land, it really would be a worthwhile effort for our local economy and our sustainability of connectivity between our home country and host country. When I travel to Bangladesh, my first port of contact will be with my home in Sunamganj. Even though I have lost many of my relatives, my parents and two brothers since leaving Bangladesh over forty years ago, I still go straight to my home in Sunamganj. Things have obviously changed since then. I no more have many friends or classmates as I used to in my home town. I do not have a single colleague in Sunamganj College where I worked as a physics' lecturer before leaving for the UK. Most of them have either passed away, or retired from their profession. I still miss my colleagues Abdu Miah, Bipresh Babu, Sitesh da, Abdul Mannan Choudhury, Nooruddin, Ranju da and others who are no more in this world. From my home, I have lost my father, my mother, my two brothers Mumit and Jahangir Bakth and my cousins Monwar Bakth Nek, Dilwar Bakth, Shahjahan Bakth and all my uncles.

Pat Schweibert quotes, 'When one person is missing, the whole world seems empty'.

I have lost so many important and close people from my life. My world definitely seems empty. And I do feel empty when I visit my home. The happy and joyous environment of living and playing together with siblings and friends is no more there. It is only the sweet memory that pulls me to visit. It is the root, the emotion, the love and belonging that pulls me like a whirlpool and compels me to visit, even though there is no one at home other than caretakers.

When I left home for the UK, friends, relatives, colleagues and students came to see me off, but now when I visit home I find it empty. My cousin Ayub Bakth Jaglu, Mayor of the local town, and my other cousins Rownak and Bahlul will welcome me, while younger brother Brig Gen Humayun, eldest sister Doctor Saleha Khatun, sister Sultana Khatun, Rukshana Khatun Lovey and Farzana Akther Jubi live in their own houses in other cities away from home. Home seems hollow. It reminds me of a quote from a headstone in Ireland: 'Death leaves a heartache no one can heal, love leaves a memory no one can steal'.

It is because of this memory, my feelings, emotions, dreams, sentimental yearning and my nostalgia that I have the wistful desire to return home in thought. No one can steal it from me.

However, my next generation are too busy working hard, making money, buying houses one after the other, moving from smaller to bigger homes and hardly having time to feel and remember their ancestral home. They are too busy with the internet, iPads, chatting on Facebook, looking for latest cars etc. I don't blame them. We have to accept reality, the changes in the family, in the society and the world.

We still remember our poor neighbourhood in Bangladesh. We collect money through community channels and send it to help those less fortunate than we are. I remember a little girl called Ayful and her little brother Siddek. Both were under the age of thirteen when I first saw them in 1970. Their parents were too poor in those days in East Pakistan, but they still had their own home, in their own village, however small it was. They were given shelter in our home by the mercy of my parents. What I still remember about these siblings is their strong bond and love for each other. Ayful used to feed her little brother herself, took care of him, bathed him and put him to sleep at night. This was something so noticeable and even my own siblings did not practice it.

Unfortunately, when war started in 1971, both Ayful and Siddek were taken back by their parents for their safety and security. Sunamganj was bombed and the panic began. People started to leave their homes and many were displaced.

After the independence, I left Sunamganj for London. Every time I returned home, I tried to track down Ayful and Siddek, but in vain. No one knew their new addresses. After nearly forty years I managed to find out where they were. I asked my contact to get in touch with them. Both of them came to see me one day. I was delighted to see them after all these decades, but was unhappy to see them undernourished, underprivileged and unhealthy. After all these years, they had failed to improve their lives. When asked why this was, they said that things had not changed since the independence and they had failed to come off the poverty line.

I had a long chat and reminded them of their childhood affection for each other. In order to help them, I gave them some money in large notes and asked Ayful to change it at the market and give half of it to her brother Siddek. Momentarily, I forgot that Ayful is now a grandma and Siddek is now an old father. They left happily and left me in my world of memories of my good old days. To my surprise, Siddek turned up the next day. He looked very distressed. I asked what had happened and he said that Ayful did not share the money with him. When I asked why, he said that she needed the money more than he did. I thought to myself that I should have given it to both of them with my own hands. Why did I make such mistake? But I remembered their young days; their love, affection and bonding. I did not know when they had severed that bond. I know it happens in the western world, because of personality clashes or childhood treats from parents.

At first, I thought may be Siddek was not telling the truth, but I tested him and was convinced that he was not lying. I gave him more money and made him happy again. He left, but it made me wonder how the financial situation of a human being could be so drastic. I remembered a quote from Mahatma Gandhi who said, 'There are people in the world so hungry, that God cannot appear to them except in the form of bread.'

I still look for people in my homeland with a poor background so that I can help them out financially, but my son who was born and brought up here and has his own house in London, would prefer to help disadvantaged Africans through charities. The good news is that I persuaded him and this year he donated his Zakat money to the poor in his ancestral home town of Sunamganj. With the help of Mayor Ayub Bakth Jaglu, I hope many more underprivileged people like Ayful and Siddek will benefit.

A Peaceful Place for Praying People

When I first set foot in Brick Lane, there was no mosque. Brick Lane Jamme Mosque was opened for prayer in 1976. Those who supported and contributed to having this mosque built were Janab Jahurul Haque, a prominent businessman from Dhaka, Janab Haji Motlib Miah Choudhury, the late Janab Goni Kari, Kadir Ali, Janab Taibur Rahman, Mostori Miah, Moulvi Arman, Isad Moulvi and others. This Grade II listed building was actually constructed as a French Protestant church in 1743. In 1819, it became a Methodist Chapel and in 1898 it was converted to a synagogue. In 1976, it became the current day mosque.

This is my local mosque, opposite my office. I have been worshipping in this mosque regularly for over thirty-five years now. It did not have a minaret before. Now the mosque not only has a beautiful 30-metre-high illuminated minaret, but also has a mihrab – a semicircular niche to show the direction of praying – and a beautiful minbar, which is a pulpit for the imam to deliver his sermon. It does not, however, have any live images or statues as these are forbidden by Islamic standards. It has occasional Quranic verses in the wall in Arabic calligraphy.

The mosque attracts a lot of foreign visitors, who respectfully take their shoes off before they enter and look around the beautiful interior décor. It's a mosque embedded with history, heritage and a hallmark of transformations. It has special architectural and historic appeal and is protected by Conservation Area status. It's a centre for social cohesion where people of other faith groups, other communities and tourists flock to see this architectural and historic building.

Recently, the mosque committee has invested a huge sum of money for its refurbishment. For the first time, this mosque now has the provisions for funeral services, which began in November 2014. It has the facility to preserve up to four bodies in its newly built cold storage.

People from far away come to pray in this mosque, or listen to Islamic speeches from renowned Islamic scholars. In the holy month of Ramadan, the mosque is totally full with worshippers, young and old. Although it can accommodate nearly three thousand people, during the holy Eid, it becomes a real problem to accommodate all at one go. However, no worshipper is left out. The mosque committee makes alternative arrangements with different prayer times to accommodate every single

Muslim. Funeral prayer also takes place regularly.

Mufti Alauddin sahib's funeral was overwhelming. He used to be the imam of this mosque. I knew him as a real gentleman, always kind, soft hearted and softly spoken. I attended his funeral (Namaj-e-Janaja), which attracted thousands of people. It was really extraordinary to witness how people travelled together to show their final respects to the late Imam of this mosque.

Once, my customer Kamal, our local boy of Wheler House, Quaker Street, who was murdered while delivering takeaway food, also attracted a large crowd in his Janaja at the same mosque where I was present too. I remember the mosque couldn't accommodate all and hence the nearby streets were used as a makeshift mat for this funeral prayer in 1997.

The funeral prayer of Alhaj Ataur Rahman Choudhury in 2015 was historic and huge. He was the President of the Brick Lane Jamme Masjid Trust Ltd and his Janaja attracted local worshippers, well-wishers, friends and community leaders who turned out early to get a seat. The mosque was over the limit and people had to queue outside to perform prayer.

Mr Ataur Rahman Choudhury will be remembered for many of his good works, including the introduction of the Muslim Funeral Service for the first time in the Brick Lane Jamme Mosque. I also attended the funeral prayer of Bongobir Col. Usmani, the late M A Rahim, Founder of the BBCC and M A Muqtadir, a great freedom fighter, and many others in our local mosque.

I saw Michael Portillo MP hitting the headlines when he visited Brick Lane Jamme Mosque in 2001. London Mayor Boris Johnson, Ken Livingstone, Ed Miliband and many other British and Bangladeshi MPs and other dignitaries also visited the mosque. The prospective parliamentary and council candidates from all political parties are given equal opportunities to address the worshippers during elections as a part of their campaign.

Brick Lane Jamme Mosque should not be seen as merely a prayer place for pious people. It's a landmark for tourists, an icon, a hub for community activities, a place for children's education, a religious and spiritual centre, a meeting point for politicians to address the worshippers and a centre of attraction and excellence too. Local boys and girls are taught not only how to read or recite the holy Quran correctly, but to learn the importance of spiritual culture and community values to earn reward in 'DEEN' and 'DUNIYA'. It's a place where good things are preached and practised and evil things like extremism are denounced. It's a place not for only one faith group, but for multi-faith communities who can assemble together, exchange their news and views, share their experiences, learn from each other, disseminate information and network.

The mosque facilitates social integration and social understanding, which are so essential nowadays for the fabric of society to remain intact. It is a place that is used not only for prayers to be performed five times a day, but also to educate non-Muslims about Islam, a religion of peace. It teaches the values of Islam, its wisdom, its belief in co-existence with mutual respect, understanding and harmony and in no way spreading or promoting hatred in society. On one side of this mosque is written 'Umbra Sumus' (We are shadows), a reference to the changes from a church, to a synagogue to the present mosque.

Brick Lane: Forty Years in the Future

I myself have witnessed many changes in last forty years in Brick Lane. Undoubtedly, the next forty years will see many more changes. But what type and scale will those changes be? At this point I will peer into my crystal ball to make some predictions about Brick Lane in 40 years' time.

My first prediction is that the number of curry houses on Brick Lane will be fewer than today. On the other hand, I have no doubt that the Bangladeshi-owned restaurant sector will survive, even though other types of restaurants will find their way into the area. However, I fully expect the curry houses to continue to dominate the dining-out market. Because Bangladeshis are not only hardworking, but very innovative, I expect talented chefs to invent new dishes that will replace chicken tikka masala and other favourites, which will attract new generations of consumers.

I also predict that the Brick Lane restaurant sector will overcome the problem of staff shortages by training a new generation of young people. I believe that more young women will become involved in the restaurant trade as they realise that it offers tremendous economic opportunities, especially for those who don't want to sit behind computers in an office all day. One thing is certain: in 40 years' time there will no longer be any language barrier between restaurant staff and customers. I also foresee that even before 40 years has elapsed, the culture of touting in Brick Lane, so prevalent in recent years, will have vanished forever.

I anticipate that ongoing gentrification will have transformed the area's traditional markets. For example, Petticoat Lane, the Brick Lane Sunday market and the dog market will all feel pain as the cityscape takes on a very new shape. Petticoat Lane market might survive because of historic reason, but markets on Cheshire Street will disappear in forty years' time.

Forty years from now, social and economic deprivation in Brick Lane will be a thing of the past. The businesses in the area will all be fully computerised and digitalised. E-commerce will completely dominate trade. Travel agencies of the future will find that almost all of their customers will buy their tickets online rather than by face-to-face contact. Additionally, because of technological innovations in the aviation sector, the time to travel between London and Sylhet in 40 years' time will be dramatically reduced. Instead of taking twelve hours, the journey will probably only take four or five hours. That said, I know for sure that future generations of British Bangladeshis will not possess the emotional connection to Bangladesh that the first and second generation migrants who came to the UK have. Put simply, the young British Bangladeshi people of 2056 will feel far more detached from their ancestral homeland than migrants like me. In any case, these young people will be very busy.

Furthermore, I expect remittances to dwindle drastically; young British Bangladeshis will invest all of their hard-earned money in homes and businesses in this country rather than sending money to Bangladesh. Perhaps, not surprisingly, this will have an effect on the many foreign exchange bureaus in and around Brick Lane. In particular, I expect that the long-established Sonali Bank, something of an economic and social landmark for members of previous generations such as me, will close in the not too distant future.

Nonetheless, young people will still retain something of their Bangladeshi identity. For example, as well as consuming pizza, fish and chips and Chinese cuisine, they will continue to eat a wide variety of traditional Bangladeshi dishes, especially when eating at home. The good news is that many vegetables used in such dishes that used to be imported from Bangladesh and other parts of the world, will increasingly be grown in eco-friendly greenhouses in Britain. I think something similar will happen in aquaculture. Instead of eating frozen fish brought from Bangladesh, new solar-powered aquaculture farms will develop around the M25, Essex and other parts of the country.

In 2015, there was only one Royal Mail post box in Brick Lane, but by 2056 I imagine that that too will have disappeared. British Bangladeshis will no longer feel obliged to send letters to their kin in Bangladesh and other parts of the diaspora – all communications will go through the internet and those yet-to-be imagined technologies. In fact, the warning signs of the communication revolution have long been evident. For example, the local post office next to Shahid Minar, near Altab Ali Park, closed and then became a Japanese restaurant. Another post office in nearby Greatorex Street received its last customer in 2014.

There will be other profound changes in ways that people communicate, as successive generations of smart phones and other mobile devices appear. One thing is for sure; the famous red-coloured telephone booths that once punctuated the streets of East London will have long vanished by 2056. By then, the only place you will be able see one is in the British Museum!

Some good news. At one time, the number of alcoholics hanging around Brick Lane and its surrounding streets was considerable. Some alcoholics were rough sleepers and were known to locals as 'methies' because of the methylated spirit they used to drink. They are long gone. Thanks go to local council for their rehabilitation.

Some bad news. Commercial landlords in Brick Lane will continue to increase rents. Those who cannot afford such high costs will be forced to leave the area. Some business people will seek opportunities elsewhere – perhaps even in London's West End where, I suggest without irony, the rents for retail and other outlets will end up being cheaper than those available in the East End. As I mentioned earlier, developers with their 'eagle eyes' have been quick to spot the financial opportunities presented by so-called uninhabitable flats and former council and housing association properties. They will buy out tenants and refurbish the properties so that they match other plush, new buildings in the area. The result will be that by 2056 many British Bangladeshi tenants will no longer be able to afford the high prices demanded by private landlords, and so they will be obliged to move to other parts of the Southeast and even further afield. Overall, I predict that in 40 years' time the once thriving, densely-packed Bangladeshi community in and around Brick Lane will have scattered and fragmented.

Some of the council properties in Brune Street are heavily populated by Bangladeshi families. Brune House, Carter House, Barner House, Wheeler House and many other Houses will be gentrified. Gentrification in and around Brick Lane has already started. Old council properties in Dongola Road, such as Bengal House, Atlantic House and few other houses in Ocean Estate have already been demolished and modern expensive houses have been built. In the future, I can only forecast that Brick Lane will not look the same again.

My fervent hope is that in the next forty years those British Bangladeshis who remain in the area will find a way out to make Brick Lane even more vibrant, more multicultural and further enhance the legacy left by members of the pioneer generations. Furthermore, given that the three current British MPs of Bangladeshi origin are female, it really is possible to imagine that a yet-to-be elected British Bangladeshi male MP will become British Prime Minister. Perhaps he will even hail from Brick Lane. As I well know, unlikely and unpredictable things can happen in politics!

Comedian and leader of 'The Crazy Gang', Bud Flanagan (1896–1968), born Chaim Reuben Weintrop, has a Blue Plaque from English Heritage with his name on it at 12 Hanbury Street, a side street off Brick Lane, commemorating the house he lived in as a child with his Polish-Jewish parents.

In 1728, Lincolnshire-born Anna Maria Garthwaite (1690–1763), the daughter of the Church of England Reverend Ephraim Garthwaite, settled at 2 Princelet Street, another street off Brick Lane, and found fame as the pre-eminent silk designer of the era. Many of Anna Garthwaite's Strawberry designs can be viewed today in the Victoria and Albert Museum. No surprise then that she too is commemorated with a Blue Plaque. It is my hope that at least one person from the Bangladeshi community who was born or lived in Brick Lane or other parts of Tower Hamlets will achieve a Blue Plaque sometime in the next 40 years.

I also hope and pray that British Bangladeshis will work with the relevant authorities to extend Brick Lane. Many visitors are not aware that Brick Lane does not start at the junction with Whitechapel High Street – this is Osborn Street – but begins just beyond the junction of Wentworth Street and Old Montague Street. For many years now, influential voices within the local community have suggested that Osborn Street should be merged into Brick Lane. I agree. It makes good commercial sense. In fact, I would go further and also recommend that Whitechapel High Street should also be absorbed, so that Brick Lane extends all the way from Columbia Road in the north to Commercial Road in the south. The new, extended Brick Lane would be fantastic attraction for visitors, creating all manner of job opportunities for locals.

Last but not least, my simple message to future members of the British Bangladeshi community in Brick Lane is to work hard and further enhance the image and legacy left by those who went before them. They should integrate with members of other communities, stay away from extremists and be good citizens. 'Live and let live' should be their motto.

Picture Says it All

London Jamme Mosque in
Brick Lane 1977

Brick Lane Jamme
Mosque in 2015

The Taj Stores
then

The Taj Stores
now

Shahnan in 1983 at 103 Brick Lane

Shahnan in 2015 at 33 Princelet Street, off Brick Lane

S B Faruk at 48 Brick Lane in 1977

S B Faruk in front of 48 Brick Lane in 2015

Shirajul Haque Shiraj in Brick Lane in 1978

Shirajul Haque Shiraj in 2015

Rajon Uddin Jalal in 1978

Rajon Uddin Jalal in 2015

Justine Ali as a child with the then PM Margaret Thatcher

Justine Ali with current PM David Cameron

Azmol Hussain Then

Azmol Hussain Now

**Nadia Ali as a child with
her parents**

**Nadia Ali with her
parents in 2015**

**Bethnal Green &
Stepney Conservative
Association in 1994**

**Bethnal Green &
Bow Conservative
Association in 2015**

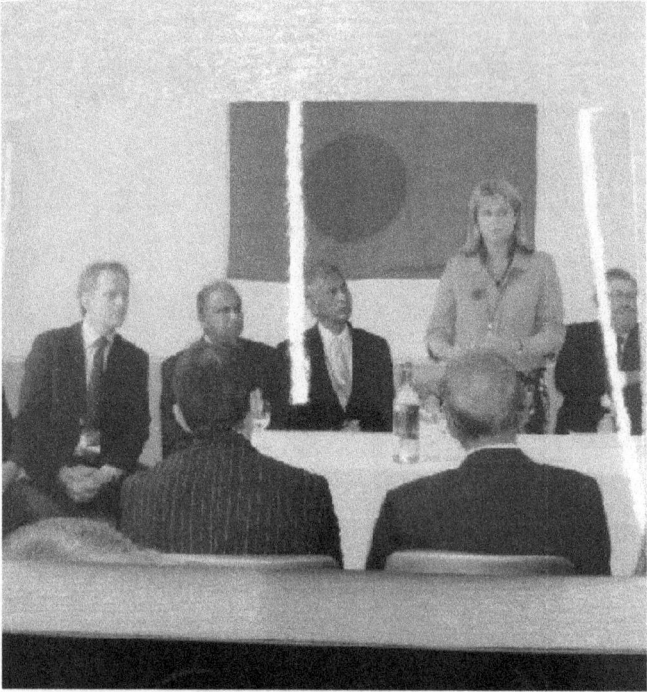

First day of the historic launching of CFoB (Conservative Friends of Bangladesh) at the Conservative Party Conference in the Marriott Highcliff, Bournemouth on Monday 2 October 2006. Anne Main MP is delivering her speech. On her right was former Bangladesh High Commissioner H E Sabih Uddin. S B Faruk is second right.

S B Faruk and his wife Sherina Faruk
with Former Prime Minister Sir John
Major and his wife Norma Major at 10
Downing Street in 1996

S B Faruk & friends with Prime
Minister the Rt Hon David Cameron at
10 Downing Street in 2014

First Citizen of Tower Hamlets Mr Abdul Mukit Chunu MBE with S B Faruk and Azharul Islam Shipar, ex VP, Sunamganj College

Baroness Pola Uddin and Zakir Khan

**Taimus Ali Goli bhai, Nijam Miah, Rafique
Ullah and others**

Tony Glover

Abdus Salique, S B Faruk and Commander Surab Ali in Brick Lane

Shah A Malique in Sangeeta, Brick Lane

**Saju Miah in front of Amar
Gaon Restaurant in Brick Lane**

**A. Shohid in his restaurant
Gram Bangla, Brick Lane**

**Shamsuddin with his invented
motorbike in Brick Lane**

**The late Haji Moinuddin Ahmed (extreme
right) and others are seen in the picture
before departing for London in 1962**

Bangladesh Journalist Association with a former Minister in Brick Lane

Olympic torch goes out from East London to Epsom

A group of barristers and solicitors of Bangladeshi origin are enjoying themselves at a party in 2015

Miss Ruje Yasmin, Journalist and News Editor of ITN, is seen here engaged in discussion with Her Majesty the Queen in 2014

A group of Bangladeshi talents in a local café after breaking fast in the holy month of Ramadan in 2015

A group of young entrepreneurs and businessmen are photographed together in 2015

Sulaman Ahmed with the Mayor of Havering and Andrew Rosindell MP at the Remembrance Day Service in Romford on 8 November 2015

Mr Monir Ahmed, Proprietor of JMG Cargo and associates are celebrating the 13th anniversary and award giving ceremony on 9th November 2015

Known faces of the community at Regency Hall, East Ham

Group of businessmen from former school, Sylhet Aided High School

Cllr Parvez Ahmed with Barrister Anis Ahmed OBE

Deputy Lord Mayor Cllr Ali Ahmed of Cardiff City

Mr Ali and Mr Kamali (below) are only two out of thousands of Brick Lane residents in East London.

Md Asaddar Ali first settled in Brick Lane in 1957. He is one of the oldest residents.

Yousuf Kamali has been a resident of Brick Lane since 1964. He is also one of the oldest residents.

Women from East End are taking part in Meena Bazar

Leaders of Jalalabad Kollyan Porishod

The President of Brick Lane Jamme Mosque Mr Sajjad Miah is seen with Mr M A Ahad, Bashir Ahmed, Mohib Choudhury and other community leaders

Thank you for reading this book. If you have never visited to Brick Lane, we look forward to welcoming you.

Afterword

Dr Sean Carey
Honorary Senior Research
Fellow in the School of Social
Sciences, University of
Manchester, Fellow of the
Young Foundation, and Centre
for London Associate

There are ordinary and extraordinary streets in the UK. The London Borough of Tower Hamlets, which has long been a unique space for global migration and socio-cultural transformation, has its fair share of streets in both categories. In the extraordinary street category I would include Bethnal Green Road, Cable Street, Commercial Road, Commercial Street, The Highway, Roman Road, Salmon Lane, Wentworth Street/Middlesex Street ('Petticoat Lane') and Whitechapel High Street. That said, it's clear after reading Faruk's fascinating book that in his mind Brick Lane is not only the pre-eminent street in Tower Hamlets, but also in the whole of East London. I tend to agree with him.

I first walked the length of Brick Lane in 1983, travelling from south to north, after I took up a research post at London University, investigating how people of different ethnicities did or did not use social space. Being a white male, I never encountered a problem with racism (or sexism) whilst walking in Brick Lane or indeed in other parts of Tower Hamlets. No one whispered or shouted abuse, threw stones or other objects, or showed me their fists or pulled out a knife. Alas, as I found out, this was not the everyday experience of many Bangladeshis and members of other ethnic minority groups in the borough.

In my interviews with locals of diverse ethnicities I discovered that, whilst people and property on Brick Lane were a target for racists in the 1970s, the street is now considered a relatively safe area. Nevertheless, Bangladeshis in particular felt that they risked racial abuse or violence if they ventured much beyond Brick Lane and adjacent estates, such as the Chicksand Estate. For instance, people told me that they considered it dangerous to walk along parts of Bethnal Green Road, especially in the vicinity of The Blade Bone pub (now the site of the popular Noodle King restaurant), a stone's throw from Brick Lane, which was a well-known hangout for National Front and later British National Party members and sympathisers. Further afield, Roman Road and its side streets, many estates on the Isle of Dogs and those in the east of the borough, were also considered problematic or even no-go areas by many Bangladeshi families.

I also discovered that because of earlier settlement in the area by Sylheti seamen (lascars employed by the East India Company), Bangladeshis from Tower Hamlets, other parts of the UK and overseas were always keen to visit Brick Lane. The street was perceived to be the social, cultural and commercial heartland of the UK Bangladeshi community. Not surprisingly, in the course of my fieldwork, I discovered that in order to minimise the risk of racial abuse or attack, Bangladeshi residents in other parts of the borough had developed specific ways and times of travelling on foot or by bus or tube to Brick Lane and other parts of Spitalfields for the purposes of shopping, meeting friends or relatives on the street or in cafés, or visiting the Jamme Masjid Mosque. Of course, even those who took considerable care could get caught out, as Faruk knows very well, since he himself was subjected to a racially-motivated attack whilst travelling by tube from Whitechapel to Leytonstone.

Over time, however, the demands of a fast-expanding Bangladeshi population meant that some brave souls were obliged to establish households in previously hostile areas in the borough. Thankfully, Tower Hamlets is now a very different and safer place from what it was when Faruk first arrived.

Although Tower Hamlets continues to suffer from a range of profound social and economic problems, (Mayor John Biggs is always keen to point out, to those dazzled by architectural, retail and leisure changes on the City fringe and Canary Wharf, that alleviating poverty and inequality in Tower Hamlets remains a considerable challenge), the borough has its fair share of success stories. Indeed, despite being one of the poorest boroughs in England, over the last 15 years or so, the educational achievements of its young people have been on a markedly upward trend. So much so that, by 2014, Ofsted categorised every maintained secondary school in Tower Hamlets as either 'good' or 'outstanding'.

Another notable success story is the catering sector. Like other people, when I first came to the East End, I was fascinated by the smells and bright neon lights of a handful of 'Indian' restaurants on Brick Lane, which were clustered around the junction with Hanbury Street. I discovered that the first Indian restaurant on Brick Lane, The Clifton, was established in 1959. Its legendary owner, Pakistani-born Musa Patel, also happened to own the freehold, not only of The Clifton, but of a large number of other properties in Brick Lane. Musa is long gone but his influence on the property market remains. Indeed, the vast majority of Bangladeshi-run restaurants and cafés serving affordable food that opened after 1977 by first or, more usually, by second generation Bangladeshis, are leased. The result is that because of steadily increasing food costs and assorted taxes, Brick Lane eateries are extremely vulnerable to the sort of rent increases recently imposed by landlords keen to exploit the area's new 'hipness'.

Like the pioneering Musa Patel, early Bangladeshi restaurateurs in and around Brick Lane felt obliged to operate under the badge of 'Indian' cuisine. As Faruk recalls, it was Abdus Salique who opened the first 'Bangladeshi' restaurant in the UK. In fact, his restaurant, Salique's, on Hanbury Street, received rave reviews for its food and decor from *Time Out* and the *Evening Standard* and became a destination restaurant, drawing customers not only from across the capital, but also from Essex and Kent. Indeed, Salique's conspicuous success encouraged other Bangladeshi restaurateurs to try something slightly different from the traditional, tried-and-tested curry house formula. So Shiraj Haque opened The Shampan and Muquim Ahmed established Café

Naz. Later they were joined by others, including Imam Uddin of Bengal Village and Azmal Hussain of Preem. At its peak in 2007, there were nearly 50 restaurants serving Anglo-Bangla food in Brick Lane and its side streets, the largest cluster of such restaurants anywhere in the world. That cluster has made an extremely important contribution to the area's regeneration. Furthermore, the restaurant boom has also provided an economic platform as well as the social impetus for the Boishakhi Mela, the Bengali New Year celebration. Remarkably, since beginning in a small way in Brick Lane in 1997, the Mela has grown into the second-largest street festival in Europe, after the Notting Hill Carnival.

I'm not really surprised, given his entrepreneurial spirit, that Faruk terminated his PhD studies in physics at Birkbeck College to join the burgeoning restaurant sector – though interestingly he did so not by opening a restaurant himself, but by becoming the first Bangladeshi in the UK to provide training in hygiene and other catering skills for restaurant owners and workers. But that decision to switch career paths undoubtedly fits well with his previous career as a physics teacher at Sunamganj College. Overall, it's clear that Faruk has made a great contribution to the prosperity of the Bangladeshi catering sector, not only in Brick Lane, but elsewhere the UK. Indeed, it's of some significance to Faruk and many others that the Indian-Bangladeshi-Pakistani restaurant sector is worth £4.2 billion annually to the UK economy – slightly more than the UK music industry, though without the music sector's political clout or influence, alas – and that around 80 percent of the sector's 10,000 restaurants and takeaways are owned and run by British Bangladeshis.

In recent years, a shortage of chefs, changes in both the day and night-time economies, shifts in consumer behaviour and the proliferation of other types of restaurant and cafés in the greater Shoreditch area, have meant that the number of curry houses on Brick Lane has decreased from its high point around a decade ago. Some Bangladeshi-owned restaurants on Brick Lane have been replaced by fashionable French, Swedish and Vietnamese restaurants. Although Faruk is very well aware of the negative impact of regeneration on vulnerable groups in Spitalfields and Banglatown, he remains an optimist about the prospects of the Bangladeshi catering sector in Brick Lane. He is confident that innovative British Bangladeshi chefs will produce new dishes to replace chicken tikka masala, the nation's all-time favourite dish, and that young British Bangladeshi women will be motivated to come into the industry. Faruk also predicts that UK-produced vegetables and fish will reduce costs, improving the sustainability of the British Bangladeshi catering sector, and that Brick Lane will remain unchallenged as the UK's curry capital for the foreseeable future. I, for one, sincerely hope that his predictions prove right, not least because Brick Lane is a shining example of an open, socially and culturally diverse 24/7 space. Faruk is rightly proud of Brick Lane's success. British Bangladeshis are right to be proud of Faruk.

Tribute of Today for Those Who were Just Like Me Yesterday and I will be Just Like Them Tomorrow

Over the last nearly four decades, many members of the Bangladeshi Diaspora, whom I knew, from Brick Lane have passed away. They had a huge connection with – and contribution for – the community of Brick Lane and beyond. I cannot remember everybody's name. However, those who died are still in my memory and I feel they deserve a mention in this book:

The late Abdul Khalik, owner of the Taj Store. He owned the Taj Mahal Restaurant in Brick Lane and Beauty Cloth Store, one of the few saree shops in Brick Lane some forty years ago.

Haji Mimbor Ali and Haji Nisar Ali, two great community leaders. They were widely known and well respected elders and leaders in the true sense.

Ahmed Fakhruddin, main architect of Banglatown and Spitalfields Housing Association died in 1988.

Ayub Ali Master, prominent from day one of his arrival and the oldest name in the community.

Abdus Sobur, a very well-known community leader and a businessman who lived at 10 Danvers House, Christian Street, London E1 1RU, and sadly passed away on 22 April 1985. He left behind his wife and children. His son, Omar Faruk, is now practising as a barrister and works from Strand Chambers.

Haji Iskandar Miah Talukdar of 45, Princelet Street. He came from village pagla in Sunamganj.

Haji Redwanul Hoque, Owner of Sonar Bangla Restaurant, 54 Hanbury Street. Haji Redwan was one of the few members of the Conservative Party in those days and will be remembered for his relentless contribution to the party and his struggle for voting rights in Bangladesh for expatriates. Sadly, he breathed his last on 21 March 2010. Although Sonar Bangla, established in 1968, is no longer there, Haji Redwanul Hoque's son, Emdadul Hoque Tipu, has been running a business from their own property under the name of Unisoft Solutions Ltd.

Kamal of Wheler House, Quaker Street, who was murdered while delivering a takeaway from Curry in a Hurry, Islington.

Haji Abdur Rahim Shikdar died in 1999. He was my immediate next door neighbour in

Princelet Street, London E1 5LP. He was a polite, humble and a pious man.

Abdur Razzak Choudhury, an editor of the weekly Prokash. He died on 4 June 1991. He was such a good, humble gentleman who always kept in touch with me. His daughter, Samantha Choudhury, is working for NatWest Bank and his son-in-law Maruf Choudhury is working for East London Small Business Centre near Brick Lane.

Haji Somsu Miah, of Brick Lane Mosque committee, a vocal and prominent community leader.

Babul bhai of Sajna Restaurant, Brick Lane who died in Bangladesh.

Alhaj A Rob, School Governor, who contributed greatly towards the creation of the collective of school governors in Princelet Street, London E1.

Haji Mohammad Jain Ullah, aka Haji Taj Ullah, lived in the Brick Lane area for forty years. I had known him since 1976. He played an important role as a Trustee of Wapping Bangladesh Association and Trustee of Wapping Noorani Mosque and Cultural Centre. Sadly, he died in a tragic road accident in August 2009. His community contribution and dedicated works are recognised in Wapping Park where a bench and tree were dedicated to him. His son, Ex-Cllr Abdal Ullah, is the founder of British Bangladeshi Power and Inspiration and campaigned vigorously in 2006 to rename 'Aldgate East' underground to 'Brick Lane' underground station.

Mr A Goni, renowned businessman of Brick Lane, died a tragic death in Sylhet while crossing a road and being hit by a truck.

Mozzommil Ali of Boratuka who lived in Wapping. His son Mamun is now a councillor of St Dunston Ward, LBTH.

Kay Jordan of SsBA. She died in December 2010. A condolence meeting was held at the Business Development Centre. It was attended by at least 250 people. The meeting was chaired by Mr Aziz Choudhury, Chairman of SsBA. I was one of the speakers and praised her industriousness and straightforward manner.

Harry owned the business next door. His corner shop was one of the oldest in Brick Lane, on the corner of Quaker Street, and was a hub for Bangladeshi shoppers. He died at the age of eighty.

Haji Moin Uddin Ahmed was the Founder of Glamour International, 48 Brick Lane, London E1 6RF. His brother, Muslim Uddin, had a shop in Hessel Street. These two brothers had entrepreneurial skills and were renowned businessmen and community leaders. Both of them have passed on.

Mr Tybur Rahman was one of the freedom fighters and the owner of a travel agency in Brick Lane. He was one of the very few people who were community leaders in the UK during the liberation war. He was with me at his last voyage from London to Sylhet. We travelled together as guests of British Airways on complementary first class tickets. We sat next to each other and had an opportunity to share many of our experiences and information on Brick Lane. He could not make his return journey and died in his own homeland Sylhet.

Mr Kari Abdul Ghoni lived at 69 Brick Lane. He died in 1994. His son Nazrul now owns two Indian Restaurants in Huntingdon, Cambridgeshire.

The late Commander Surab Ali died in Bangladesh. He was buried with full military honours in the presence of many dignitaries as a renowned freedom fighter. His sons are now running his restaurant in Brick Lane. The late M A Muqtadir, freedom fighter and the late M A Rahim, Founder Chairman of the British-Bangladesh Chamber of Commerce. Their funerals were held in Brick Lane Jamme Mosque.

Maulana Mufti Alauddin Sb, Imam Brick Lane Jamme Mosque. He died in January 2011. His funeral at Brick Lane Jamme Mosque was attended by a large congregation of mourners who came from all over the country. He is survived by his sons Badrul and Sadrul.

Maulana Sadikur Rahman, former Imam of Brick Lane Jamme Mosque, who said goodbye to me in front of my office at Princelet Street before going for pilgrimage to Holy Mecca. He died and was buried there. His family is still in London.

Mozid Miah of Modern Saree Centre, Brick Lane. His sons moved the shop to Green Street, Forest Gate and are doing well in competition with Indian business rivals.

Alhaj Abdul Matlib Choudhury, Founder of Dil Chad Restaurant, Widegate Street, whose son, Alhaj Ataur Rahman Choudhury, was the President of Brick Lane Jamme Mosque. His other son, Mr Shafiqur Rahman Choudhury, is an MP in the Bangladesh Parliament. Azizur Rahman Choudhury and Abdul Hamid Choudhury look after Dil Chad Restaurant near Brick Lane.

Dr Bashir Ahmed, Founder of the Surma newspaper, Haji Tera Miah of Notun Din and Nurul Islam of Janomot Newsweekly.

Haji Monir Uddin of Chattak died in London in 2011 of old age. His funeral was held also in London.

Haji Monaf passed away in 2014. He was my good neighbour in Princelet Street and his son also died a premature death. His other son Moinul looks after their restaurant in Brick Lane.

The Mayor of Tower Hamlets, Monir Ahmed, who was also a classmate of my elder brother.

Mayor Abdus Salik of LBTH.

Aminul Haque Badsha, a freedom fighter and journalist passed away in Orpington Hospital on 9 Feb 2015. His Namaj-e-Janaja was held at Brick Lane Jamme Mosque on 13 Feb 2015. He was flown to Kustia to be buried near the grave of his mother.

Alhaj Ataur Rahman Choudhury, President of Brick Lane Jamme Mosque, died of a heart attack on 15 April 2015 at St Thomas' Hospital, London. His Janaja was held on Friday 17 April at Brick Lane Jamme Mosque. The mosque was full to its capacity, so many mourners had to perform the Janaja outside. The Vice Chairman of the mosque, Mr Sajjad Miah, Ex-Councillor and the son of late Alhaj Ataur Rahman Choudhury, delivered a very emotional speech and many worshippers came close to tears. Mr

Choudhury was a very soft-spoken gentleman who respected others. He had improved several facilities and developed the mosque in many ways, including the introduction of the Muslim Funeral Service. I stayed in the same hotel in Mecca and Madina while we performed the holy Hajj together with his families. He was such a good man. He was laid to rest near his mother's grave in his own village in Bangladesh.

Haji Asaddar Ali, Vice Chairman of SsBA, died of cancer on 9 September 2015.

I will miss you all.

RIP.

Recommended Resources

BOOKS

Rahman, S. (2012) Lascar. Historical fiction. Indigo Dreams Publishing

Ullah AA & Eversley J. (2010) The Bengalis in London's East End. Swadhinata Trust

Chatterji, J. and D. Washbrook (eds). (2013) Routledge Handbook of the South Asian Diaspora. London and New York: Routledge

Visram, R. (1986) Ayahs, Lascars and Princes: Indians in Britain, 1700-1947. London: Pluto Press

Visram, R. (2002) Asians in Britain: 400 years of history. London UK and Sterling VA: Pluto Press

Kershen, Anne J. (ed.) (2015) London the Promised Land: The Changing Migrant Landscape in Early 21st Century London. Ashgate Pub Co.

Forman, C. (1989) Spitalfields: A Battle for Land, London

Choudhury, Y. (1993) Roots and Tales of the Bangladeshi Settlers. Sylheti Social History Group

Leech, K. (2006) Doing Theology in Altab Ali Park. Darton, Longman and Todd Ltd

Rahman, U. Bilate Bangla. (Feb 2015). Sahitya Prakash

Rahman, U. (2007) Brick Lane: Bileter Bangalitola. Sahitya Prakash

Burstein, D. (2010) London Then and Now. Batsford Ltd

Shuckburgh J. (2003) London Revealed: Uncovering London's Hidden History. Collins

Albera, D. and Eade, J. (eds). (2015) International Perspectives on Pilgrimage Studies: Itineraries, Gaps and Obstacles. Routledge

Maxwell, P. (2014) Photography Book of Brick Lane. Spitalfields Life

Eade, J. Tales of Three Generations of Bengalis in Britain. (2006) Swadhinata Trust

OTHER PUBLICATIONS

Janomot Newsweekly
The Weekly Desh
Surma Newsweekly
Notun Din
Potrika
Spice Business Magazine
Curry Life Magazine
East London Advertiser
Brick Lane Newspaper
Bangla Mirror
Bangla Post
Bangla Sanglap
Euro Bangla
London Bangla
Jummabar
Weekly Bangladesh
Weekly Bangla News
East End Life
Who's Who
Darpan Monthly Magazine
Millennium Post
Muslim Index (2010)
Shomoy
UK Bangla Directory (2003)
Ken Leech and the East End of London 1958-1998, Jubilee Group Paper

WEBSITES

www.towerhamlets.gov.uk
www.visitbricklane.org
www.bricklanebookshop.org
www.swadhinata.org.uk
www.thebricklanegallery.com
www.bricklanejammemasjid.co.uk
www.eastlondonmosque.org.uk
www.timeout.com
www.group.canarywharf.com
www.ideastore.co.uk
www.stratfordlibrary.org
www.richmix.org.uk
www.geos.ed.ac.uk
www.philmaxwell.org
www.open.ac.uk

RECOMMENDED PLACES TO VISIT

ALDGATE: Aldgate near Brick Lane has a history that goes back 700 years or more. It is said that this 'OLD GATE' was used by Romans to travel to their capital, Colchester in Essex.

Aldgate Pump is in the junction of Fenchurch Street and Leadenhall Street and this point was used from 1700 to measure distances into the counties of Essex and Middlesex.

Aldgate is right on the edge of the City of London Corporation. It is situated on the famous square mile radius of the affluent City. The nearest tube is Aldgate and connected with the Circle and Metropolitan lines.

Today it has multiple high rise buildings, insurance offices and banks etc., which has changed the landscape.

The Gherkin and Guildhall are within walking distance from Aldgate.

ALTAB ALI PARK: The park is named after Altab Ali who was murdered here in 1978. You can see a beautiful monument known as 'Shohid Minar'. The park has seats to relax and enjoy the green surroundings and open space. It can easily be reached by tube, bus or on foot.

The nearest tube stations are Aldgate East and Whitechapel. Both have Hammersmith, District and City Lines.

BRICK LANE JAMME MOSQUE: Situated at 59 Brick Lane, this historic building is a must for visitors to visit. However, permission is needed to gain access as there are certain prayer times when visitors are not allowed in.

The nearest tube station is Aldgate East and the nearest overground station is Shoreditch.

BRICK LANE BEIGEL BAKE BAKERY: It is open 24 hours and serves traditional Jewish-style filled bagels such as salt beef and smoked salmon. It is at 159 Brick Lane and within walking distance of Shoreditch station and tube stations Aldgate East and Bethnal Green (Central Line).

COLUMBIA FLOWER MARKET: The end of Brick Lane merges with Columbia Road and this is where you'll find the world famous flower market and other shops, established in 1869, which are open every Sunday.

DENNIS SEVERS' HOUSE is in Folgate Street not far from Brick Lane. It is a 'still-life drama' created by the previous owner as a historical imagination of what life would have been like inside for a family of Huguenot silk weavers.

It is a Grade II listed Georgian terraced house in Spitalfields. From 1979 to 1999, it was occupied by Dennis Severs, who gradually recreated the rooms as a time capsule in the style of former centuries. It is now open to the public.

EAST LONDON MOSQUE: East London Mosque is a stone's throw from Brick Lane at: 82-92 Whitechapel Road, London E1 1JQ. The nearest tube stations are Aldgate East, Aldgate and Whitechapel. Buses: D3, 25, 254, 205

SPITALFIELDS CITY FARM: Anyone wishing to visit a farm and see farm animals near Brick Lane should visit Spitalfields City Farm. The farm was set up by volunteers in 1978 and receives over 18,000 visitors a year on its 1.3 acres of land. It is in a colourful, vibrant and multicultural area.

THE GEFFRYE MUSEUM OF THE HOME is located in Shoreditch just minutes from Brick Lane. It is easily reached by public transport. The nearest stations are Hoxton and Old Street. Address: 136 Kingsland Road, London E2.

HANBURY STREET: Hanbury Street is just off Brick Lane. It has its own history. In the seventeenth century, Hanbury Street was known as Brown's Lane after the original developer. For nearly three hundred years it has been known by its present name, taken from that of a local family who owned the land.

Jack the Ripper murdered his victims at 29 Hanbury Street in 1888. No. 29 has been demolished, but that sensational murder is still in the history books.

Hanbury Street also hit the headlines in 1999 when a nail bomb exploded in Brick Lane. The bomber had originally left the bomb in a bag in Hanbury Street. A member of the public found the bag and took it to the nearby police station in Brick Lane. As it was Saturday and the police station was closed, he put it in his car boot. However, realising the bag might contain a bomb, he abandoned his car near to the police station. The bomb eventually exploded injuring six people and destroying the nearby cars and restaurants Café Naz and Sweet and Spice.

Kobi Nazrul Centre is at 30 Hanbury Street, serving the community as a flagship arts and cultural centre, which hosts community events and festivals.

Brady Arts and Community Centre is at 192-196 Hanbury Street and is a home to LBTH Arts, Parks and Events Service and 'A' Team Arts, who provide art classes and workshops to young people. Nearest tube stations: Whitechapel, Aldgate East. Buses: 25, D3, 254, 106

IDEA STORES: In addition to a traditional library service, Idea Stores offer a diverse range of adult education classes, career support, training, meeting areas and cafés and arts and leisure pursuits. Address: 321 Whitechapel Rd, London E1 1BU. Nearest tube station: Whitechapel.

JOHN WESLEY'S HOUSE is a small Georgian house built in 1779 by John Wesley. He lived there for the last twelve winters of his life and provided a home for the preachers of the Chapel, their families and servants. The house still contains many of John Wesley's personal possessions and furniture, including his electrical machine and study chair. Methodists the world over consider Wesley's small Prayer Room to be the Power House of Methodism. Address: 49 City Rd, London EC1Y 1AU

KENSINGTON GARDENS: Kensington Gardens covers 265 acres and was originally part of Hyde Park. It is the home of Kensington Palace, the birthplace and home of Queen Victoria until she became Queen in 1837. Address: London W2 2UH. Opening times: 6am – 9pm

KEW GARDENS: The world's most famous botanic garden, just half an hour from Central London. www.kew.org. Address: Royal Botanic Gardens, Kew, Richmond, Surrey TW9 3AB. Opening times: Open daily from 10am. Closing times vary. Closed Christmas Eve and Christmas Day.

LEE VALLEY REGIONAL PARK: This award-winning park stretches 26 miles along the River Lee. It comprises regional sports centres, urban green spaces, heritage sites, country parks, farms and nature reserves.

The Lee Valley Regional Park Authority also owns three London 2012 venues. At its southernmost tip is Trinity Buoy Wharf, which is a thriving centre for the arts and creative industries. It has an experimental lighthouse, built in 1864, while the largest surviving tidal mill in Britain (c. 1776) can be found at Three Mills Island. www.visitleevalley.org.uk Address: 64 Orchard Place, London, E14 0JY. Opening times: Free access to open spaces. Times vary for individual attractions.

V&A MUSEUM OF CHILDHOOD: This museum in Bethnal Green has the largest collection of childhood objects in the UK. The museum was founded in 1872 as the Bethnal Green Museum. The Museum displays a variety of collections at different times. Address: Cambridge Heath Rd, London E2 9PA. Nearest tube station: Bethnal Green (Central Line).

NATURAL HISTORY MUSEUM: A world-class visitor attraction, which cares for more than 80 million specimens. Address: Cromwell road, London SW7 5BD. Nearest tube station: South Kensington and Gloucester Road (District line)

OLYMPIC STADIUM: Queen Elizabeth Olympic Park, Stratford, London E20

OSMANI PRIMARY SCHOOL: Vallance Road, London E1 5AD. Walking distance from Brick Lane. Nearest tube station: Whitechapel

PRINCELET STREET: Princelet Street is just off Brick Lane. 19 Princelet Street, close to Brick Lane Jamme Mosque, is a unique cultural institution, in one of London's most beautiful historic buildings. Built in 1719, it has been a refuge for Jews and was originally used by Huguenots escaping persecution in France. It is now a museum to all the East End's immigrants, including Sikhs and Bengalis. Visitors and supporters of the project include those who have fled from Burundi, Somalia and Kosovo.

Although not often open to the public, group visits can be organised.

PETTICOAT LANE MARKET consists of two adjacent street markets, which have over a thousand stalls selling clothes and household goods. Wentworth Street Market is open six days a week and Middlesex Street Market is open on Sundays only. It is only five minutes' walking distance from Brick Lane.

QUEEN ELIZABETH OLYMPIC PARK: Only 2.7 miles from Brick Lane, this is the city's newest park, covering 560 acres. It

encompasses one of Europe's largest urban shopping centres, some of the finest restaurants and a range of attractions to appeal to everyone. Tube stations: Nine tube and train links (Central Line, Jubilee Line).
Buses: Numerous. A map showing all local bus services is available at
www.tfl.gov.uk/?cid=pp004
www. queenelizabetholympicpark.co.uk/

RICH MIX is only few minutes' walk from Brick Lane. It is East London's independent arts venue. They have spaces for creative businesses, three cinemas and a multitude of flexible performance spaces. Shoreditch is the nearest overground train station.

OLD SPITALFIELDS MARKET is one of the most famous, popular, old and historic markets in the United Kingdom. It is located close to Brick Lane and dates back to 1638. Stalls range from contemporary and vintage fashion to music, toys jewellery, accessories and home interior items. Nearest stations: Aldgate East (District Line; Hammersmith & City Line), Liverpool Street (Central Line, Circle Line, Metropolitan Line, Hammersmith & City Line)

TOYNBEE HALL was created in 1884 by Samuel Barnett and his wife Henrietta for future leaders to live and work as volunteers in London's East End. This would enable them to come face-to-face with poverty, giving them the opportunity to develop practical solutions. A couple of the individuals who came to Toynbee Hall were Clement Attlee and William Beveridge. Toynbee Hall has been working as a catalyst for social reform in the UK for 130 years and continues to create new ways to help those who find themselves in poverty, even today. It is two minutes' walking distance from Brick Lane.

UNIVERSITY OF EAST LONDON (UEL): The University of East London is within the London Borough of Newham. It is a cosmopolitan university attended by students of many nationalities from the local area and overseas. It's a good place to watch the planes take off from London City Airport in Dockland.

VICTORIA PARK falls in both the boroughs of Hackney and Tower Hamlets. It is one of London's most important and oldest public parks, which has been visited by millions of Londoners for nearly 170 years. The park is the largest of all the London parks, covering an area of 86.18 hectares and attracts around 9 million visitors a year.

A wide range of formal and informal sports, sponsored activities, events and festivals including Bangladeshi Boishakhi Mela take place throughout the year. Address: Victoria Park, Grove Road, Bow, London E3 5TB. Nearest underground station: Mile End (Central Line, District Line, H/C). Nearest overground stations: Cambridge Heath/Hackney Wick

WHITECHAPEL GALLERY: Founded in 1901, the Whitechapel Gallery has a history of firsts. In 1939, for example, Picasso's iconic depiction of the horrors of the Spanish civil war, entitled Guernica, was displayed in the gallery on its first and only visit to Britain. The gallery is famous for its exhibitions of modern and contemporary art, in addition to its education and public events' programmes.
Address: 77-82 Whitechapel High Street, London E1 7QX. www.whitechapelgallery.org Opening times: Tue to Sun, 11– 6pm; Thur 11 – 9pm. Closed Mondays.
Price: Free, with a charge for special exhibitions. Tube station: Aldgate East (District Line and Hammersmith and City)

YORK HALL is a health and leisure centre and one of Britain's best known boxing, gym and swimming venues. The venue is situated on Old Ford Road in Bethnal Green and within walking distance of Brick Lane. The hall first opened in 1929. The nearest tube station is Bethnal Green.

ZSL LONDON ZOO is within walking distance of Camden Town and Regent's Park stations and a short bus ride from Baker Street station. Address: ZSL London Zoo, Regent's Park, London NW1 4RY. www.zsl.org/zsl-london-zoo

www.ingramcontent.com/pod-product-compliance
Lightning Source LLC
LaVergne TN
LVHW091251080426
835510LV00007B/218